Babe Ruth's lifetime record of 714 home runs was presumed the ultimate, never to be surpassed. Then, in 1971, 37-year-old Hank Aaron hit 37 homers and suddenly loomed as the one man who could—and did in 1974—hit more than the Babe.

Aaron's record is well known, but the man remains a mystery. Behind his careful mask of casual calmness is one of the most unusual personalities in sports—he fought his way out of poverty to become not only a top player on the diamond, but one of the most mature of men off it.

Now, for the first time, the story of Henry Aaron is told with the insight and vivid immediacy that it deserves. We can see who Hank Aaron really is—what it took and how it felt to chase a ghost to prove his claim to greatness.

HANK AARON:
The Man Who Beat the Babe
by Phil Musick

An Associated Features Book

POPULAR LIBRARY • NEW YORK

PHOTO CREDITS

Cover—Ken Regan (Camera 5)

UPI—pp. 10, 13, 19, 25, 56, 70, 80, 88, 91 (bottom) 97, 105, 116, 119, 152, 171 (bottom) 202, 211, 213 (bottom) 216

Ken Regan (Camera 5)—30, 35, 174, 186, 197, 221

Dennis Smitherman Collection—45, 50, 91 (top), 134

NBC-TV—171 (top), 213 (top)

To a Babe named Russell,
who, alas, helped raise
a singles hitter

Acknowledgments

Behind every author—in addition to a good woman and the Mittyesque desire to make them forget Shakespeare—stands dozens of people without whose assistance he would not be an author.

Since I am no exception, I'd like to offer a sincere word of thanks to those who made this project both possible and as painless as might reasonably be expected.

Sandy Musick steadfastly held the family fort, and, as usual, served without yawn as sounding board and gentle but honest critic. And two unsinkable blondes, Kristi, 7, and Keri, 5, once more suffered the sacrifice of their Dad to the Smith-Corona with no more complaint than an occasional, "Do you have to work in the basement, again?"

This book was conceived by Zander Hollander of Associated Features and he suffered its completion under pressure with the wit, capable guidance and professionalism that are as much a part of him as his mustache.

The keepers of the morgue at the *Atlanta Journal* and *Atlanta Constitution* were patient and helpful, as was Jim Schultz of the Atlanta Braves, who provided coffee, cordiality and his Hank Aaron files.

I would be remiss in failing to thank Wilt Browning, public relations director of the Atlanta Falcons. In a period of more dignified employment, he was an excellent baseball writer for the *Atlanta Journal* and his insights into the subject were incisive and helpful.

Certainly, no one provided greater assistance toward the completion of the book than Judy Anderson, super-secretary, who typed the manuscript, singled out its more obvious flaws with an unflagging smile, and never once observed that she was being spectacularly underpaid for her help.

Contents

1. 715   11

2. The Cross-Handed Dreamer   26

3. A Shy Clown   39

4. A Break from Bobby Thomson   55

5. "Is That Really Robin Roberts?"   68

6. "I Just Want to be Known as a Singles Hitter"   81

7. The Beer Went Flat . . .   93

8. The Pride of a Loner   107

9. Black Enough   121

10. The Avis Approach   133

11. Hank's Mental Bank   148

12. Topping Willie   163

13. Living with a Ghost   175

14. Wait'll Next Year   187

15. Move Over, Babe   203

715: The shot that dropped the Babe to No. 2.

1

715

It was a moment—a series of moments, really, punctuated by the word "history" flashing through your consciousness—to hold in the mind's eye for all of time. A moment to roll across the tongue, to grip with each of the senses. A hot ash of a moment that flamed and died far too soon, so that you longed to bring it back and relive its many nuances over and over.

But, mostly, a moment to store in the frontal lobes against those days far removed when you knew you would, from time to time and relishing each telling, say "Yeah, I saw it. Yeah, I remember it like it was yesterday. Yeah, sure, I remember Hank. The Hammer, we called him. Yeah. Sure."

A moment to bank, so that in the winter of life it could be drawn forth and waved proudly in the face of disbelieving youth; a piece of proof that, indeed, there had been the good, old days and you had been a part of them.

A series of moments, some blurry, some etched in memory. The ball—five ounces, nine inches in circumference, cowhide, marked with the numbers 12-12-2-2 in indelible ink, an immortal artifact now—flashing up and out through the misty rain. Dodger leftfielder Bill Buckner scrambling desperately up the bullpen fence and then hanging there in futility. Al Downing, wheeling and firing the fastball that rose invitingly into Henry Aaron's power zone until it met the wicked counterforce of his bat. Aaron striding toward first base, eyes never leaving the ball. Aaron down-shifting into his home run trot as he realized the ball was beyond Buckner's leap. Aaron's jivey hand slap to Dodger second baseman Davey Lopes. Two teen-aged boys accompanying him on the joyous circuit. Aaron grinning when thunderous boos fell upon Monte Irvin, there to represent an afraid Bowie Kuhn. Aaron choking slightly on the words "thank you ... thank you ... thank you, I just thank God it's all over." Aaron, eager to be done with the celebration, asking "Is that all? Is that all?"

Aaron. Not Ruth. Aaron. Just plain, old Henry Aaron. At the top. All by himself. Looking down on Ruth and all the rest from that loftiest of perches, 715. A statistic, 714, and a name, Ruth, now subservient to a new number and a new name. So did Babe Ruth join Dempsey and Palmer and John L. in whatever repository exists for legends who have outlived their day.

At exactly 9:07 p.m. of an overcast, windy and cool April 8th evening in that turbulent year, 1974; with one man on base, the count 1-and-0 and Los Angeles shifting uncomfortably atop a 3-1 lead over the Atlanta Braves; in front of a standing-room-only crowd of 52,780 screamers come to see history—and one notable absentee; against a dramatic backdrop of controversy and conflict, and off a 32-year-old veteran of 13 seasons of pitching who ironically also wore the No. 44 on his back; did Henry Louis Aaron, that noble, aging gentleman out of Mobile in his 21st big-league summer, conquer the most

Babe Ruth, 1924, on the way to his homeric mark.

impressive sporting statistic of them all. In the process, he survived excruciating pressure, added to his stature as a man of uncommon pride and dignity, and lent new meaning to the word consistency.

The historic day had dawned cloudy over Atlanta. Five Points, the busy heart of the city, was festooned with big, green posters announcing an event of major importance. "Dogwood Festival," the posters read, "April 6-14." As usual, Atlanta was unmoved by its most celebrated citizen. Yawned a man leaning against a Peachtree lamppost, "Aaron and Watergate, that's all we've been hearing for months. I think folks are good and tired of it." At the plush Marriott Hotel, only 150 of the Braves 400 fan club attended a luncheon at which Aaron reportedly was to attend. A block away, in front of the graying pillars of the Atlanta Union Mission, a toothless, black derelict offered the opinion, "That's Georgia for you. It takes a lot to get them excited, and it's not much of a baseball town, anyhow."

Evidently, Bowie Kuhn agreed. He had decided rather than attend the Atlanta-Los Angeles game of April 8th, he would accept an invitation to appear at a cocktail party-dinner at the Cleveland Stadium Club, being held in honor of the Indians' owner. Kuhn had been expected to be in Atlanta and throw out the first ball, a chore later jointly and effortlessly handled by Henry Aaron's parents. "I had no commitment to be there," Kuhn countered. He had courageously forced Aaron to play in two of the first three games in Cincinnati, thus triggering a controversy that reached the height of ridiculousness when Georgia congressman Dawson Mathis, D-Albany and champion of the intrinsic right of Atlantans to witness the crushing of Ruth, said in response to the order Aaron play against Cincinnati, "I think it is time for Congress to take another look at organized baseball."

14

Perhaps aware he might collar the votes of the Georgians who would later decorate Atlanta Stadium with banners reading "Hank 714 Bowie 0" and "Phooey on Bowie," Dawson described Kuhn's edict as "the most tyrannical and unreasonable thing I ever heard of."

No one in Atlanta was happy with Kuhn's gutty order to Aaron and the Braves—quite possibly the reason he did not show up. But home run 715 remained a marketable item for the commercially-minded Braves. After hitting the home run that tied Ruth's record on his first swing of the season in the April 4th opener in Cincinnati, Aaron gave a feeble imitation of himself in the third game of the series against the Reds on April 6th. He struck out twice—on a total of six pitches and twice taking called third strikes—and tapped out feebly to third base, and Atlanta got its chance at history. And Estella Aaron—who had been unable to go to Cincinnati because of an illness—got her chance to see her son become immortal.

"She keeps saying, 'Henry will wait until I get to Atlanta to break the record,'" Herbert Aaron Sr. chuckled shortly after arriving at Atlanta Stadium on the eventful night. "She says, 'he wouldn't do it without me there.'" Speaking for herself, Estella Aaron said indignantly, "I don't like the way they're treating my boy and you can put that in big letters so that Mr. Commissioner will know how I feel."

Most of the Aarons were there. The wispy but energetic father and the stout, outspoken mother were accompanied to the park by their three daughters and eldest son, Herbert Jr. Herbert Sr. used the time before a lavish pre-game ceremony honoring his son to reminisce. "He made it for himself. He made his bat talk. Henry is cool. I've always been cool," rambled the 65-year-old former shipyard worker. "I seen a lot of trouble in the shipyard, but it don't bother me. You teach a dog how

15

to hunt, he'll hunt. But he needs teaching."

Meanwhile, the subject of Herbert Aaron's educational skills sat in the Atlanta clubhouse. The press that had hounded him for months was still there, but hitting the 714th had lessened the tension Hank Aaron felt. "It used to be nobody bothered me, and I didn't bother nobody," he said, chuckling. "I'd hit three homers, there'd be no reporters around. Now they're around every day."

And so they were, in the hundreds, overflowing the regular pressbox and cramming into an auxiliary one hastily constructed by the Braves along the right field line. Like most people in Atlanta Stadium two hours before the nationally-televised game began, they paused to note such celebrities as Sammy Davis Jr. and fanatical Braves' fan Pearl Bailey, who would sing the national anthem after observing excitedly, "Ain't seen nothing like this since the burning of Atlanta. All we need now is to see General Sherman and a bunch of Union soldiers come charging in from left field."

In fact, the pre-game ceremonies had everything else: exploding cannons; hundreds of multi-hued balloons thrust into the night sky at the same instant; 38 teen-age lovelies in white mini-skirts with Aaron's 44 emblazoned on their blouses; a huge American flag in the shape of the United States painted on the outfield turf, and to top it off, an enactment of the *This Is Your Life, Henry Aaron.* Introduced to the fans, who later applauded wildly whenever he was visible, Aaron was characteristically terse. "I just want to thank all of my friends for being here. I'm just hoping this thing will get over with tonight."

With that the scoreboard flashed, "Go, Hank." That was Hank's intention. Before the game he determinedly told a friend, "I'm going to get this over with very quickly."

Al Downing, of course, had a different idea. When

Aaron came to the plate to lead off the second inning, Downing was feeling the pressure. He had given up Aaron home runs Nos. 674 and 696 and he had been interviewed at length about the possibility he would permit No. 715. "I don't want to be the guy," said Downing, hoping to pitch the Dodgers' fourth straight complete game. "If he does hit it, I wouldn't feel any disgrace...and I wouldn't feel any pride." Giggling nervously, he added, "Of course, the ideal situation would be to have a 6-0 lead in the ninth inning."

But the situation was not ideal; the game scoreless. Downing worked ever so carefully and the bat never left Aaron's shoulder. Downing missed the outside corner with a curveball, hit it with a fastball and then, perhaps sobered by the experience, was wide with his next three offerings and Aaron walked, eventually scoring the game's first run on Dusty Baker's double and an error by Los Angeles' left fielder Bill Buckner. It was Aaron's 2,063rd run scored, moving him ahead of Willie Mays as the leading scorer in National League history and into third place behind Ty Cobb and Ruth on the all-time list. The crowd was unimpressed with the records, hooting Downing unmercifully and perhaps contributing to the record-breaking home run.

Although the Dodgers had staked him to a 3-1 working margin in their half of the third inning, Downing seemed disconcerted when Aaron next appeared at the plate in the bottom of the fourth inning. Leadoff man Darrell Evans had been safe when shortstop Bill Russell juggled his routine groundball a moment too long and perhaps Downing was irritated. In any case, he missed the outside corner with his first pitch as Aaron watched impassively and later Guy Bush, who had issued Ruth's 714th, thought "he looked like he figured he had to get the next pitch in there because the crowd had been on him."

Whatever the motivation, Downing came with a fastball as dozens of fishnets fought for air space with gaily-colored umbrellas in the outfield stands. Aaron leveled the 34-ounce, Del Crandall-model Louisville Slugger, stepped into the pitch and snapped those marvelous wrists. Only Downing—"I didn't think it would carry"—ever had a doubt concerning the ball's ultimate destination. A drive of perhaps 415 feet, it disappeared beyond Buckner's reach into the Brave bullpen just to the right of the 385-foot marker. Atlanta reliever Tom House raced for the back wall of the bullpen and leaped, stretching his 5-foot-11 frame to its full extent. The ball caught in the webbing of his glove, far below the reaching hands of paying customers hoping to pick up the 25-grand bounty entertainer Sammy Davis had placed on the ball earlier in the day. Ironically, had it not been for House, the ball would have hit a huge blue-and-white sign carrying a message from the First National Bank: "Think of it as money."

Atlanta Stadium exploded, literally, as it became apparent Bad Henry had just given his ultimate answer to the crazies who had threatened his life in their hate mail when he began his final run at Ruth. Two days later, a fan said of the wild, wild applause, "it was deafening, I can still hear it." Fireworks screamed their technicolor delight across the purplish sky. Huge, stark, white block letters six-feet high lit up the centerfield message board, shouting 715 before a trigger-happy operator in the control booth switched to *HANK*. An auxiliary message board held the jaunty order, *Move Over, Babe. Here Comes Henry*. The Dodgers—who committed six errors—entered into the spirit of the moment with handshakes.

When Aaron reached the plate, grinning widely now, Ralph Garr was there to help him plant his foot on home plate and the Braves, untrammeled joy lighting their faces, hoisted him to their shoulders briefly. But a thin,

18

These fans will be able to say they helped
Hank tour the bases on his historic blow.

Atlanta relief pitcher Tom House retrieved the 715th
and turned it over to Aaron.

laughing black man, who had leaped from a box seat near the Atlanta dugout and outrun the young Braves to the plate, had a previous claim. And no one pounded Hank Aaron's broad back with quite so much glee as did Herbert Aaron Sr.

As Aaron moved to a spot 20 feet from the Atlanta dugout to pose for photographers and receive ceremonial gifts, Estella Aaron rushed through the crowd of milling bodies and hugged her son, to be replaced seconds later by a deliriously-happy Billye Aaron. House, who had led the rush from the Atlanta bullpen, the ball clutched tightly in his fist, handed Aaron the greatest prize of his career as his wife clung to him. In the background, Atlanta president Bill Bartholomay and Commissioner Kuhn's representative, Monte Irvin, waited patiently as Aaron posed smiling, hat tilted askew over his right eye, for the cameras. When a gap opened in the ranks of the photographers, Aaron stepped to a microphone and quietly said what he had been saying all along, that he was glad it was all over.

Bartholomay presented Aaron with a diamond-encrusted ring featuring replicas of himself and Atlanta Stadium, and engraved with words calling him "a great ballplayer and fine gentleman." Irvin stepped to the mike and was introduced as Bowie's alter ego. Fittingly, the crowd rained its displeasure down upon Irvin, who handed Aaron a solid-gold wristwatch with diamond face-numerals worth $3,000 and tried unsuccessfully to outshout those who had no use for his boss. "Thank you very much, Monte," Aaron said, but he grinned when the first boos fell.

The game was delayed for 11 minutes and when it resumed, no one was particularly interested. By the time the White House attempted to get in touch with Aaron—"I'm sorry, he's in the outfield," a Nixon aide was told by the stadium operator—more than 60 telegrams had been sent to the stadium and 20,000 fans, saturated by history, had gone home. Aaron went into the clubhouse between innings to take Nixon's congratulatory call and was invited to visit the President at his convenience—moving a pressbox wit to observe, "Yeah, even in jail."

Too soon, for most, the night ended. The Braves won, 7-4, although no one including the Braves seemed to care much. Dodger manager Walt Alston's worse fears had been realized. Before the game he said, "I know he's going to hit it sooner or later, but I hope it doesn't cost us a ballgame." Providing a 3-3 stalemate and firing the Braves' desire not to tarnish the occasion, it did. There were some small ironies. Downing was a former Yankee; Aaron's first home run had been off another ex-pin striper, Vic Raschi, and on this night he was wearing a pair of baseball shoes discarded by a third Yankee, one-time Brave Joe Pepitone. An earlier Aaron prophecy had been proven correct. Of the pitcher who would become the goat of 715, Aaron had said "he won't be a rookie or some borderline guy . . . he'll have to have the guts to challenge me with his best pitch." Downing wasn't a rook or a fringe pitcher; and the pitch that carried him into baseball lore was a fastball, a strength he was willing to pit against Aaron's strength.

Unfortunately, before the game had even ended there were the inevitable apples-and-oranges comparisons between Ruth and his successor. The arguments—silly because time and changes in the game had rendered comparison impossible—usually were reflected in the age of those extolling them. The oldtimers saw Aaron as an interloper who had merely managed to blot out Ruth's magnificence because of his durability. Aaron needed 2,967 games to hit No. 715; Ruth had authored one less in 464 fewer games, or a shade over three seasons as they

21

were numbered in his days. Ruth hit a homer in every 11.8 official at-bats; Aaron's ratio was one every 15.9 appearances. Aaron had 2,700 more at-bats. Ruth "wasted" four years as a pitcher. Aaron was hitting a livelier ball. And on and on.

Aaron's champions countered with their own statistics, interpretations. Aaron averaged 3.1 more home runs per year than Ruth did. Ruth was never tormented by the multitude of night games and lights which blind the hitter to the bottom half of the ball; or the drain of jet lag. Ruth was home-run conscious from the outset; Aaron only when the opportunity to create a new record came into view.

Yankee and Atlanta Stadiums entered the fray. The ball fairly leaps out of the park in Atlanta, crowed the Ruth fans. Aaron supporters countered, yeah, but Yankee Stadium with its short, low right field stands, yawning invitingly, aided Ruth, and what about the home runs he bounced into the stands? And on and on.

Perhaps the man most moved by the occasion—Aaron seemed more relieved than overjoyed—was Tom House, who had retrieved the historic ball. A bespectacled relief pitcher living on the bare edge of a job in the major leagues, he could barely describe his feelings. "I couldn't believe it," he said. "This is the biggest thing that ever happened to me. When I'm old and have grandchildren, I can say I was on the other end of the 715th home run."

Actually, he'd had it all the way. Before the game began, his confidence bolstered by having caught No. 687 on the fly, House told Aaron he would catch the ball and bring it to him. No, he said later, it never occurred to him to retain it because it wore Sammy Davis' $25,000 price tag.

"Buckner was yelling 'lemme have it . . . lemme have it,'" House said. "He and I chatted about it before the game and he said to me, 'If we get it, do we get to keep it?' I told him I really didn't know. We, I mean the Braves, made up our minds we were going to give it back to Hank."

And so House did. "He said 'thanks, kid,'" House recalled, "but I don't know if he knew it was me. I remember him making eye contact with me over his mother's shoulder."

Someone asked House if he'd had second thoughts about returning the ball. "Not one bit. You have no idea the feeling it gave me. I felt super.

"It meant a whole lot to me. I've been a fringe ball-player all my life. I was just hoping I could make the club this spring so I could see the man do his thing."

Having done his thing, the man's immediate thoughts were of accusations that in the third game at Cincinnati, he had not tried to hit the record-breaking home run; had yielded to the Braves' desire to capitalize on history.

"I have always tried to do my best," he said, some anger in his voice. "There was a lot of criticism about my performance but (Clay) Kirby made some good pitches on me and that's all there was to it.

"I have never went on a ballfield and not given my level best. Contrary to some of the reports I have read that I was a disgrace to the ballclub, I did my level best."

Some reporters shuffled their feet as Aaron spoke of his future. Yes, this was his last year, but before it ended he was "thinking about that career average of mine. What is it? .311 or .312? Now I can concentrate on trying to do something about that."

He chided Kuhn, but did not lash out at him, although he could have done so with impunity. "I'm glad it came in Atlanta . . . I felt it would have been courteous to have let me wait to try to hit it here."

Ultimately, the topic became his retirement. Would he

want to be the first black manager? "I'd take the job if it were offered, but I really don't want to manage. I feel I could do more helping out in our farm system."

In fact, Brave president Bill Bartholomay could one day soon give baseball some of the dignity it's lost by failing to hire a black manager, because Mathews has not produced and Atlanta has a history of shuffling managers. "My admiration for Hank goes beyond description," Bartholomay had said. "He's Mr. Brave. Any route he decides to take will have my full support. All he'll have to do is tell us."

A wire service reporter called Mrs. Claire Ruth, the Babe's widow, in her New York apartment and, like Downing, she was a bit sad. "I sent Henry a wire that covers everything. The Babe loved baseball so much I know he'd have been pulling for Hank." The reporter's questions drew little response other than that, and he finally hung up and Claire Ruth turned on the television set to watch her husband's record washed away on the 11 o'clock news.

While Claire Ruth was watching an endless stream of instant replays on the news and a guy was remembering Hank Aaron one time saying "once I walk out on that field when there's forty or fifty thousand fans who came to see my play, I don't like to let them down," Herbert Aaron's eyes were filled with nostalgia.

". . . he was 14 . . . a shortstop . . . couldn't run too fast . . . but he could hit the ball."

Yeah, even then.

"I'm thankful to God it's all over."

2

The Cross-Handed Dreamer

The vintage Greyhound, as weathered and tired and scarred as the old man but as resolute as the boy, lurched off the road in front of the country store, sighed its relief and lunged to a stop. The men, half-awake, stumbled into the Carolina sunshine. They did not look like clowns. They wore the bone-weary, unshaven, wrinkled look of barnstormers, but some of their luggage carried the word "Clowns." And, indeed, they were the Indianapolis Clowns, although often they laughed about how few of them had ever been in Indianapolis. The Clowns were a traveling baseball team, like the Homestead Grays and Kansas City Monarchs and a half-dozen other lesser-known aggregates. Riding the dusty backroads of baseball, they bided precious time until the nation shook its unease at seeing black pitchers bring it high and tight under white chins and spikes on black feet bite into white calves.

Life for the Indianapolis Clowns was not funny. A game in Wichita, 24 hours in the tired, cramped bus, a game in Louisville. The bus. Chattanooga. The bus. Memphis. Back in the bus. Life was two dollars a day meal money; $200 a month salary. And talking endlessly about "that Robi'son boy up in Brooklyn." And bologna and crackers and Twinkies and Pepsi. And, on Saturday night, a broken-down bed in a broken-down hotel. But, always, the bus.

Henry Aaron didn't mind. His eyelids fell when the wheels turned one rotation; rose grudgingly when they ground to a halt. Preacher Jenkins didn't mind, either. He had known worse times.

When the bus pulled up in front of the country stores that served as the Clowns' restaurants, the lanky nomadic pitcher would buy the bologna and bread that were the staples of his diet. Later, he would sell half the loaf of bread to a teammate.

The boy who usually rose beside him was oblivious to food. He ate to keep up his strength for the game. That was what was important, baseball. The game wasn't so important to the older man. Survival, that was his game. Everyday he would meticulously remove a dollar bill from his wallet, put it into an envelope and lick it closed.

"Why you doin' that?" the boy asked once.

"Mailin' it to my wife," the older man said. "I send her half my meal money every day."

The boy nodded. He understood about being poor.

Months before, the boy, Henry Aaron, had left Mobile, Alabama, with two dollars, two sandwiches, an extra pair of pants, a cardboard suitcase and his mother's heart, to seek all the fortune the Indianapolis Clowns could afford to bestow upon him.

Listening to his wife sob as the third of his eight children walked toward the train that would carry him north to the Clowns' training camp, Herbert Aaron was uneasy and knew a sense of foreboding. But quickly he put them aside.

If the boy stayed in Mobile, what sort of life could he expect? Herbert Aaron made $75 a week as a boiler-maker's helper in the Alabama Shipyards. When he retired 20 years later, he would be making $115 a week. Long before Henry Aaron was born, his father had lost any illusions he once might have had concerning what life held for an uneducated black man in the south. Years before, he and his wife had escaped the numbing futility of trying to scratch a living from the hardscrabble farms of Wilcox County.

Mobile, 125 miles and many light years dead south, was where you looked for the rainbow if you were black. And if it hadn't been, as the song proclaimed, "a heaven by the name of Mobile," it still beat hell out of Wilcox County. A man could find work in the shipyards along Mobile Bay, and if that work kept him away from home for long stretches of time, still it put food in his kids' bellies. And Toulminville wasn't nearly the worst of the shanty towns which huddled together between the city and the bay. And Estella kept the place neat, the kids clean and respectable, and food on the table. Still, thought Herbert Aaron, it was probably better that the boy go. Maybe he would find a richer, easier life.

Playing baseball guaranteed it. From the time Henry Aaron could remember, it was all he wanted. "He didn't have many friends," Estella Aaron said. "He was so interested in baseball, he didn't have time for them." When he was 40 and a legend in pursuit of another, baseball would remain pretty much all that Henry Aaron wanted.

Even the day of his birth—February 5, 1934—had come on a day important to baseball. Hundreds of miles from where Estella Aaron was giving birth to a lusty, bawling 10-pound boy named for his paternal grandfather, the troubled National League had taken a new purchase on life. A swaggering, hard-drinking lout named Ruth, wielding a sort of power with the bat never seen before, had captured the baseball fans of America for another league. But on this day, wealthy Powell Crosley Jr. had agreed to pump new money into the National League by buying the Cincinnati franchise.

Herbert and Estella Aaron took little note of the National League's problems. They had their own, magnified by the Depression. Three of their eight children were infants—Herbert Jr., Sarah and Henry. Five more would be born in short order—James, Tommie, Alfredia, Gloria and a boy who died in infancy.

The Aarons' world extended only from Toulminville to the docks of Mobile Bay. In Chicago, a gangster named Al Capone sensed the end of Prohibition and the streets of the Loop ran red with the blood of his would-be competitors; in Austria, a maniacal paperhanger was screaming the words that would plunge the world into a war which would one day force mankind to question its sanity; in Mississippi, the sight of a black man hanging from a telephone pole did not necessarily unnerve whites. But little beyond Toulminville touched the family of Herbert Aaron.

The Aarons lived quietly, their energies channeled along the path of "making do." Herbert Aaron made 18 cents an hour as a shipyard laborer during the Depression, but lacked the training to exploit the prosperity brought later by the Second World War. Quiet, unassuming, uneducated, Herbert Aaron worked, talked baseball with his friends, attended the Baptist church, reared his children sternly but with affection, and accepted life for what it pretty much was—hard. A man worked hard, was honest, sucked what enjoyment he could from his existence, taught his children right from wrong, persevered, provided "enough to eat...clothes" so that no Aaron "would go begging." And he accepted some hard facts. Life was no picnic. When Herbert Jr. smashed a tin can with a broomstick into the side of his brother's head,

29

As a youngster, Hank Aaron played on this field in Mobile, Alabama, revisited by Hank in 1973.

slicing it wide open, their father advised Henry to remove his face from his mother's skirt. "Take it like a man."

Another fact of life was segregation, and Herbert Aaron taught his sons to accept it. One-third of the 190,000 people who called Mobile home were black, but it was a city hard on blacks. When integration finally could be staved off no longer, Mobile responded to the opening of its public schools by organizing a record number of private, all-white ones. But Herbert Aaron was too busy with economic problems to spend much time worrying over political ones. Herbert Jr. earned $25 a week packaging groceries in a market, Sarah a similar wage doing housework. There was a garden behind the house and Henry tilled it. "It was a struggle, but we got along," he would say later.

From the time he was four and would follow the older kids down to Council Field, Henry Aaron played baseball. It consumed him. "I had a taste for it in my mouth that never went away." Ted Blunt, now a Mobile policeman, would stop to watch the kids' games on his way home from work and laugh at the four-year-old staggering around with an unwieldy glove on his left hand. "But even then, Henry threw a baseball like a man, not a little child."

Baseball. Estella Aaron. School. The library. They were the stuff of Henry Aaron's life until the day he climbed aboard a train that would carry him off to the Negro leagues and beyond.

"He was a quiet boy," Estella Aaron remembered. "He liked to stay in and read a lot. Mostly he read comic books, things about sports. He read a lot about Jackie Robinson. He was a boy who liked to be by himself."

In fact, Henry Aaron was never alone. If he had few friends, was "a Mama's boy who liked to hang around the kitchen," he always had a ball. Herbert Aaron would

31

roll rags together and tie them with string. Henry would fire the rag ball into the sky and run to camp under it as it fell. When that palled, he would go to the side of the house with a rubber ball and a stick. "He'd throw the ball onto the roof and when it slid down, he'd hit it against the side of the house with a broom or mop handle," Herbert Aaron said. "He'd do that over and over. The only time I remember him getting into trouble was for cutting the top off his mother's new mop. He got a good whupping for that."

Lean and lank at 10, Henry Aaron wore out rag balls, rubber balls, stones and even bottle caps with his mother's mop handles. "If Henry wasn't home, I knew he was over at the park playing ball," Estella Aaron said. "That's all he ever wanted to do. If all children were as easy to raise as Henry, a lot of mothers would have fewer gray hairs."

Came the summer of 1945 and most of the people of Toulminville knew that if you wanted Henry Aaron, he would be the skinny kid hitting cross-handed and playing short at the recreation center a block from his house, or slapping the tongs on a 25-pound block in the back of the ice truck that toured the neighborhood late each afternoon.

The world was cooling down in Henry Aaron's 11th year. Mushroom-shaped clouds appeared over two Japanese cities, the Austrian paperhanger destroyed himself, and Johnny came marching home again. In August of 1945, in a graying stone building at 215 Montague Street in Brooklyn, another Johnny was preparing to march off to a new war. Branch Rickey, baseball's prime mover and shaker, had dropped a bomb on the baseball world by signing a black player. Jackie Robinson affixed his name to a contract on August 29, in a stroke putting the first real crease in the game's color line and firing an idea in Henry Aaron's 11-year-old mind.

Two years later, Robinson the pathfinder would come to Mobile in a Dodger uniform and Herbert Aaron would escort his son to the ballpark "to keep him from being trampled." Watching Robinson, all grace and fire and power and dignity, Henry Aaron told his father, "I'm going to be like him. Before he's through playing, I'll be up there with him."

If it would be a while before Henry Aaron and Jackie Robinson played on the same field, they shared one thing in common: Prejudice. When it came time for Aaron to attend high school, he was assigned to Central in Mobile. From Edwards Street, you walked 10 miles north to the black high school nearest Toulminville, passing through neighborhoods full of white children singing the popular litany of the day, ". . . grab a nigger by the toe." At 15, Henry Aaron was too rangy, his glance too unwavering to be subjected to racial taunts. But no one had to tell him about injustice. He could see it in the paved streets and stately magnolias and shiny cars of the white neighborhoods. "On the way to school, the others would be attacked by white kids and I read about some of the girls being attacked by white fellows, but I never knew about such things myself."

It would be years before a man named King began driving a way of life named Jim Crow out of the south, and in 1948 Central High School was no worse than other black schools. There, Aaron played softball—the school didn't have a baseball team—and football, and Florida A & M offered a scholarship to the lithe, quick quarterback with the big arm.

There was little about Central High that attracted Aaron. "The teachers were old and our library was very poor." He especially did not like class. After all, what did an isosceles triangle have to do with hitting the inside pitch to right? Estella Aaron knew little of either, but she knew the way out of Toulminville could be discovered only in school. She didn't mind Henry fishing and swimming in Mobile Bay; she was delighted when he spent hours at the library; she didn't even mind a little baseball, as long as it wasn't Sunday. But she was adamant: Henry Aaron would get an education.

One does not, however, get an education in a poolroom, and when he was 16 and had cut school 10 days running and been caught staring at a tough bank shot by his father, a crisis developed.

Herbert Aaron had played some baseball himself and understood the drag it could have on a boy. But not even Estella Aaron revered education as much as her husband. Father and son sat in the family auto and held a council.

"You don't think these fellows playing in the big leagues are dumb, do you?" Herbert Aaron asked.

"I was listening to a baseball game in the poolroom," his son explained. "Brooklyn was playing. I want to be a baseball player, and I'll learn more about playing second base listening to Jackie Robinson play on the radio than I will in school."

For two hours they talked, the boy with his dream, the man with his reality.

"Son, I had to quit school because I had to go to work. You don't have to. Every morning, I put fifty cents on your dresser for you to buy your lunch and whatever else you need. I don't take but twenty-five cents to work with me. It's worth more to me that you get yourself an education than it is for me to eat. You aren't going to drop out of school until you're through."

The decision had been made. Henry Aaron went back to school, suffering the boredom it brought him with the aid of baseball. Scraping up ground balls for the Prichard Athletics, a team in a nearby town, Henry Aaron attracted, as he would again and again, knowing eyes. He was, in a word, a natural. The way Ava Gardner smiled and Ben Hogan hit an eight-iron, that's the way Henry

Hank's in the kitchen with his mother Estella and his dad Herbert, who once took 13-year-old Hank to see Jackie Robinson play in Mobile.

Aaron played baseball. He needed no instruction. He was one of those monstrosities the sandlots often produce—a cross-handed batter—but once he was persuaded to desist, the rest came with the ease of flowing water. He could never remember any other coaching save being told "always throw overhand."

At 16, the talent came leaping out of him. Maybe it was the nonchalant way he flipped the ball, the way it came squirting out in a leisurely arc from a point very near his right hip but always arriving at first base just ahead of the runner. Or maybe it was the way basehits crackled from his bat in an endless stream, or the controlled grace that, even when he was playing with older boys, always seemed to dominate a game and draw attention.

Ed Scott wasn't a baseball man, but he didn't have to be to see that Henry Aaron was something special. He watched the 16-year-old Aaron play one game and made an offer. "Kid, how'd you like to play baseball and make some money doing it?"

Scott had a good friend named Billy Tucker, who ran the Memphis Black Bears, a semipro team that had once employed Satchel Paige and often played the teams of the Negro American League. But the Bears played on Sundays; Estella Aaron didn't hold with Sunday baseball.

"It's not every kid that gets a chance to play for the Memphis Black Bears," Scott persisted. "I'll see," Henry Aaron told him.

But he knew it was hopeless, and for three consecutive Sundays when Ed Scott came to the white frame house on Edwards Street, Henry Aaron hid. Finally, Aaron could stand it no more and on the fourth Sunday, he and Ed Scott prevailed over Estella Aaron's better instincts.

Billy Tucker, a neighbor of the Aarons, knew he had struck paydirt immediately. Henry Aaron made the jump to semipro ball without a hitch. Estella Aaron still questioned her decision. "Some of those players are twenty-one or twenty-two. Some of them have families."

Age was the only thing Henry Aaron gave away to his new teammates, and after a few weeks, he got a raise to $10 a game. After particularly impressive outings—he fought the ball some at third base, but even then hit with power—Mrs. Billy Tucker would give him a bonus. "I want to do something extra for you," she would say, withdrawing a couple of dollars from her purse.

He was 17 and he could hit it for distance and run and throw; owned the basic skills a scout prizes above all others. At five-foot eleven, 155 pounds, the only thing he lacked was size. His lack of stature, and one scout's pre-occupation with it, parlayed to prevent Aaron and Jackie Robinson from one day becoming teammates. At a Brooklyn tryout camp, a Dodger scout glanced briefly at Aaron and turned his attention to other prospects. "He told me I was too small," Aaron recalled. "He sent me home."

Bunny Downs made no such mistake. Front man, traveling secretary, major domo, scout, he was all things for the Indianapolis Clowns. When the club came to Mobile to play the Black Bears on the final day of the 1951 season, Downs watched a kid infielder handle Indianapolis pitching with ease, singling twice and legging a third single into a double.

"How old you, kid?" Downs asked after the game.

"Seventeen."

"You still in school."

"Yessir. I graduate next year."

"You always play short?"

"I play anywhere they want me to play."

Quiet kids who hit and "play anywhere they want me to play," weren't all that plentiful. "How would you like to play for the Clowns?"

"I don't see no reason why not."

"I'll send you a contract next spring."

Being poor often makes a man a cynic; being poor and black guarantees cynicism. "I never thought I'd see the guy again," Henry Aaron told a friend. "Then there was the problem of trying to convince Mama I was old enough to leave home. So why not say 'why not?' "

Autumn gave way to winter, winter to spring. One day an envelope postmarked Indianapolis arrived in Mobile. The Clowns' owner, Syd Pollock, was offering Aaron $200 a month to play baseball. He showed the contract to his parents, and got the biggest surprise of his young life.

Estella Aaron beat back her fears and nodded. She did not understand the lure of baseball, but if that was what Henry wanted . . . Herbert Aaron understood the attraction, but he remembered making 18 cents an hour. He picked up the fallen gonfalon of education. "My father said no," Henry Aaron said. "He wanted me to go to college." Estella Aaron prevailed. "He was so young . . . I worried for him. But that's all he wanted, to play ball. So I let him go."

The pursuit of Babe Ruth had begun.

3

A Shy Clown

They looked at him and prodded each other in the ribs and mostly they laughed. This skinny kid, this woe-begone, silent, big-eyed black waif with his five-year-old spikes and his raggedy-ass glove and his five-dollar suit, this kid was going to be one of them? This kid was going to play in the demanding Negro American League, with its tough veterans and tortuous schedule and petty jeal-ousies and closed ranks? This kid, who for God's sake, swung cross-handed was going up there against Satchel and Smoky Joe Williams?

No one leered harder than Buster Haywood, who man-aged the Indianapolis Clowns. Syd Pollock, he thought, must be going crazy. Hell, this kid couldn't even talk. And look at the way the veterans shouldered him out of the cage after he'd taken only a couple of licks. Hay-wood shook his head. This rook wouldn't last out the week. On the day the Clowns opened training, Haywood told the equipment man to give them all warmup jackets to ward off the morning chill. Forget the kid, Haywood said. He wouldn't be around long enough to get cold.

So on those June mornings the wind would whistle down across the western slopes of the Blue Ridge Mountains 30 miles to the east and cut cleanly through the cotton uniform that hung on Henry Aaron the way a pup tent would've hung on a skinny Christmas tree.

He spent the mornings shivering. Winston Salem, N. C., is cold in the spring. Delicate whitecaps often form on the middle fork of the Muddy Creek River, which swings south of town before meandering its way out of the northeast corner of North Carolina. But the weather was not the only thing that chilled Aaron. None of his new teammates did more than nod at him occasionally, usually with humorless smiles. "They treated me like I was a disease. A new player meant one of the older ones had to go." Buster Haywood wasn't so sure. And neither was Henry Aaron; a premonition he'd had the day he left Mobile seemed to be coming true. He had left home with little more than a thin hope of success. Estella Aaron had given him "all the money I had, two dollars and two sandwiches in a brown paper bag." The rest of the family had spent their tears. "Ma, Pa, Sis, my brothers, they practically carried me on the train. I was scared they'd get on and go with me. We all cried pretty hard. I didn't really expect to last long with the Clowns."

Buster Haywood knew a similar foreboding. His camp was jammed full of veterans, old and wise and hardened against a hard life. This stripling, he knew, would never make it. "Won't be too long before we get rid of some of these green kids and get our team down to size and start hitting the big towns and seeing some sights," Haywood would say in a stage voice when Aaron was around, winking at the older players. Aaron spent most of his time absorbing insults—"Hey, kid, where'd you get that equipment, the Salvation Army?"—and waiting for the axe to fall.

But when the Clowns' season opened in Chattanooga, he clung to the roster. In the few opportunities Haywood had given him, Aaron demonstrated that he could use the bat. Throughout late spring, the Clowns traversed the country and Henry Aaron sat on the bench, acquiring on a two-day sojourn to Buffalo a reputation for somnolence that would remain with him throughout his career. "He fell asleep when he got in that bus in Kansas and I don't think he wake up until we get to Buffalo," a teammate marveled. "Then he get off that bus and get ten hits in eleven times at bat."

Few people consider Buffalo anything but Paradise Lost. When President McKinley was assassinated there, those who had spent any time in Buffalo nodded knowingly. For decades the city has been second to Pittsburgh among targets for comedians in need of a civic gag. What finer location, Buster Haywood thought, to apply the coup de grace to a rookie? In the opening game of a doubleheader against the talented Kansas City Monarchs, Haywood put Aaron in the lineup for the first time. He hit the third pitch of his professional career into the street that ran behind the left field fence. He followed the homer with a sharp single and a pair of ringing doubles. In the second game, he had six straight hits and started five doubleplays. Before the day ended, Haywood had discovered a new respect for youth, the team's most respected veteran, Ray Neal, had nicknamed Aaron "Little Brother," and visions of a bonus began dancing in the head of a Boston Braves' scout named Dewey Griggs, who had witnessed the display.

"One thing bothers me," Griggs told Aaron after the second game. "You throw everything sort of underhanded. Can't you throw overhand?"

41

"Yessir. But I warmed up cold—I don't have a jacket—and I didn't want to hurt my arm."

"Get this kid a jacket," Griggs roared.

Haywood provided a jacket and Syd Pollock offered some batting instruction. He had been no less impressed than Griggs, and the years had honed Pollock's instincts for the dollar. Syd Pollock made a buck with the Clowns, but for owners of black baseball teams, the scuffle never ceased. Rainouts, broken crankshafts, boozing pitchers, infielders waylaid by silken women, they all cost Syd Pollock money. This lanky shortstop out of Mobile who did his talking with the bat might just pay for a lot of broken crankshafts. If Griggs was interested, would not other scouts be? Immediately, Pollock took a personal interest in Henry Aaron. "Switch your hands around and hit the regular way," he ordered.

The orthodox grip was not comfortable, but as the Clowns wandered through the East, Aaron hit nearly .500 and attracted birddogs other than Griggs. "I wasn't completely converted," Aaron said. "If I got two strikes on me and my back was to the dugout so they couldn't see, I'd sneak my left hand back on top."

The placement of his hands seemed to matter little. In a month's time, Aaron's .467 average was high in the Negro American League and Syd Pollock was getting a warm feeling all over every time he saw a major-league scout.

Through the grapevine, a New York Giant scout from Puerto Rico, Pedro Zorilla, heard about Aaron. Zorilla, who would later uncover a jewel named Roberto Clemente, made contact with Pollock. The Clowns' price tag on Aaron, $7,500, dampened Zorilla's interest only slightly and negotiations began. Meanwhile, Pollock needed some money to meet his payroll and dropped a letter to John Mullen, the Braves' farm director, who had helped with such problems in the past. The letter had a postscript that was pure bait: "We got an eighteen-year-old shortstop hitting cleanup."

In the space of a few days, Griggs reappeared and Zorilla made a concrete offer. The Giants would settle with Pollock and pay Aaron $250 a month to go to Sioux City, Iowa, in the Class A Western League.

At Griggs' insistence, the Braves counterpunched. "This kid's worth $7,500 just for his swing," Griggs told Mullen. "I'd make the down payment out of my own pocket. Play him anywhere you want to—he can do anything but pitch and catch. But don't do anything to him at bat. He's one of the finest natural hitters God ever put on this earth."

The Braves topped the Giant offer and a deal was struck. Pollock would get $2,500 down; $500 if Aaron made an AAA league; the full $7,500 if he reached the parent club. Aaron would get zilch for a bonus; $300 a month to play for Eau Claire, Wisconsin, in the Class C Northern League. As they later would with Clemente—"he strikes out too much," sniffed owner Horace Stoneham—the Giants would not boost their offer. A matter of $50 a month prevented Aaron and Willie Mays and any warm body from forming one of the finest outfields in baseball history.

Naive concerning front-office machinations, Aaron was little more than a pawn in the negotiations. "Inside I was busting wide open I was so excited. But I was never the excitable kind, so I acted like I wasn't paying any attention." Still, when Buster Haywood tried to dissuade Aaron from signing with Boston, he was told with a leer: "No, Buster, you really ought to get rid of some of these green kids and hit the road and see some sights."

But inattention to the bargaining cost Aaron considerable money and later he would say bitterly: "I always felt some people took advantage of a poor, black kid who didn't know any better."

This was the age of the six-figure bonus. Months before, Pittsburgh signed kid smoke-thrower Paul Pettit out of Southern California for 110 grand. Henry Aaron, proven in a demanding brand of baseball, got a cardboard suitcase and an airplane ticket to Eau Claire. "If I'd been one of those smart kids, I'd have said I'd go with the team that made me the biggest offer. I didn't have to go with the one that made Syd Pollock the best deal."

The negotiations were consummated when the Clowns reached Charlotte, North Carolina, and Aaron was pointed in the general direction of the airport. His introduction to organized baseball was not particularly auspicious. "I rode that plane like it was a bronco. I was shaking and trying to keep from throwing up all the way to Wisconsin." In a week, he was ready to go home.

Bill Adair, a former major leaguer who was managing and playing second base for Eau Claire, was no more impressed with Aaron than Haywood had been. Until, of course, he watched the youngster hit. And in his first few weeks in Eau Claire, that's all Henry Aaron did. Hit and sleep in his room at the YMCA. Eighteen days after his arrival, Aaron was hitting .400 and Adair, a quiet Alabaman, didn't know what to make of his new superstar. "No one can guess his I .Q. because he gives you nothing to go on," Adair wrote in one report. "He sleeps too much and looks lazy. Not a major-league shortstop prospect yet, but as a hitter, he has everything in the world."

Henry Aaron didn't think he had much of anything in Eau Claire, and the day before he was named to the all-star team after only 18 days in the league, he packed his cardboard suitcase and placed a phone call to Mobile to notify of his impending arrival.

"I'm homesick . . . I'm coming home," he told Estella Aaron.

Aaron's older brother, Herbert, Jr., grabbed the phone. He had been an outstanding athlete, but during a time

It's 1952 and that fellow at far left, middle row, is Hank Aaron of the Eau Claire, Wisconsin, Bears.

when baseball would not accept blacks. He felt a keen sense of loss.

"Man, are you out of your mind?" he asked Aaron. "Don't make a fool out of yourself. I just wish I'd had the chance you have."

"Well, come up here yourself if you think it's so great."

"Henry, don't make a mistake. If you come home, that's what you'll be doing. I know you're homesick. But see if you can't stick it out."

Henry Aaron said he would try. For a little while. The next day Adair informed him he'd been voted the all-star shortstop. "That was a real shot in the arm," Aaron said. "Something to get my mind off being homesick and some other things that were bothering me. I was a long way from Mobile . . . playing with white fellows for the first time. That bothered me. But when I made the all-star team, it gave me a feeling of belonging."

In fact, Henry Aaron did not belong in Eau Claire. At least his bat didn't. Settling into a comfortable groove at mid-season, he flat wore out Northern League pitching. And his personal life improved. There were two other blacks at Eau Claire and they roomed with Aaron at the YMCA. Wes Covington, older and acknowledged leader of the trio, was a free spirit who would later play for five major-league teams and earn the nickname "Kingfish" because, as Aaron put it, "he was always shooting off his mouth." Covington and a catcher named Julie Bowers made life a bit easier for Aaron, and he led the league with a .336 average in 87 games and was its MVP.

"It was very good, very good at Eau Claire," he said. "I didn't experience anything out of the way there, any racial trouble at all. I had a lot of white friends. People invited me to their homes for dinner. There was this one white girl. I didn't date her, she was just a friend. She used to have me over home with her parents for dinner and we'd sit out on the porch in old rocking chairs and talk and look at the stars. It was the first time I'd played ball with whites and it was quite an experience for me."

"He was eighteen years old, but he looked about twelve," said a writer who covered the Northern League. "He was so shy that you had to pity him. Yet you could tell he was going to be a star just from the way he carried himself."

The parent club figured from the way that Aaron carried himself at shortstop, he was going to have to play another position. He had continued to flip the ball with an underhand motion that might've sufficed in the Northern League but would've been an insurmountable handicap in better competition. Before the season ended, the Braves dispatched Billy Southworth, a former Brave manager and now a scout, to Wisconsin to evaluate Aaron.

"Henry, have you tried to throw the ball any other way, sidearm, or maybe overhand?" Southworth inquired. Aaron said no. The flaw was correctable, Southworth thought. "Well, I was just wondering, that's all. I like the way you handle the bat; just keep it up."

Returning to his hotel room, Southworth immediately dashed off a letter to the Braves' general manager, John Quinn: "Aaron has all the qualifications of a major-league shortstop. He runs better than average, so I would have to call him fast, but not very fast.

"He is a line-drive hitter, although he's hit a few balls out of the park. He has quick hands, gets the ball away accurately. He gets a quick jump on the ball and can range to his left and right. I saw him go far to his right into the hole and he came up throwing and virtually shot his man out going to first. . . .

"For a baby-faced kid of eighteen years, his playing ability is outstanding."

When a more detailed report was submitted by Southworth, Quinn studied it and made a decision. Henry Aaron would train with the Braves the following year. There, he would be tutored in hitting by Tommy Holmes; converted into a second baseman by another Brave minor-league manager, Ben Geraghty. Undoubtedly, Aaron was a prospect, but he had shown himself an unorthodox player, and baseball worships nothing more than orthodoxy.

Shortly after his 19th birthday, Aaron reported to the Braves' camp at Bradenton, Florida. Holmes' mouth tightened as he watched Aaron in the batting cage. A onetime manager of the Braves, Tommy Holmes had for a decade been one of baseball's most feared streak hitters. In 1945, he hit safely in 37 consecutive games, a National League standard that has remained intact. Holmes held some unyielding beliefs about hitting, and young Henry Aaron unknowingly was trampling them. He was a free swinger, hitting the ball where it was pitched. After an exhibition game in which he had hit two home runs, Aaron was elated. He had come to Florida expecting to remain with the Braves when they broke camp and went North—"I'd never had trouble making any team before"—and the home runs strengthened his belief he would open the year in Boston. The following day, after a conference between Holmes and farm director John Mullen, Aaron suffered a rude awakening.

"He doesn't pull the ball," Holmes had told Mullen with a grim look. "He'll never be a big-league player."

"You really don't think he can make it?"

"Not a chance, the way he pushes the ball."

Mullen informed Aaron of Holmes' slightly less than prophetic opinion. For the first time in his brief pro career, Aaron showed emotion. "Send me to Waycross then. I'm not going to get a chance here." The Braves' farm teams trained in Waycross, Georgia, and, reluctantly, Mullen acceded to Aaron's request.

Aaron hit the ball viciously throughout the spring and Holmes' ability to judge raw young talent became increasingly suspect in the Brave organization. But Holmes' edict brought delight to Geraghty, who managed the Jacksonville Tars of the Class A South Atlantic League, the club to which Aaron had been assigned.

Ben Geraghty was a rawboned Irisher with a horsy face and a jaw so sharply pointed it could've been used to etch glass. He had played shortstop for Brooklyn a dozen years before. Above all else, he enjoyed Schlitz beer and baseball, and if there was a prejudiced bone in his body, Aaron never discovered it. Geraghty watched Aaron rain basehits across Florida during spring training and immediately asked that he be sent to Jacksonville. There was, however, a problem. No black had ever played in the Sally League; indeed, none had ever played in the south on a regular basis, the Southern Association remaining lily-white until the day when it suddenly went bankrupt and disappeared.

"You'll be the first," Geraghty told Aaron. "Does that bother you?"

"I don't guess so," Aaron replied. Being first at anything couldn't be too bad, he reasoned.

"It won't be easy," Geraghty said. He knew the Sally League well, knew that in towns like Montgomery, Alabama, black players would be viciously taunted. "It won't be easy... you've got to know that. But I sure want you."

Geraghty got Aaron and two other black players, Felix Mantilla, a firebrand from Puerto Rico destined for the majors, and Horace Garner, a rangy centerfielder who would never leave the minors.

Aaron was still the naïve young man who had been swindled out of his bonus money. Playing in the south

49

Aaron, left, and Felix Mantilla broke the color line in the Sally League (along with Horace Garner) when they played for Jacksonville in 1953.

would not be easy, he knew, but he had a plan to make it easier. "Be good ... be so good they can't remember what color you were when the season began."

Aaron was that good, but his bat could not hide his pigmentation, even though he was hitting nearly .400 midway through the season. Aware that his talents had outstripped the Class A level, he relaxed in spite of cruel treatment by white fans. He was smilingly shy around the clubhouse and became the butt of good-natured abuse from his teammates. Before games, Geraghty often would find him asleep on a pile of equipment bags. He was 19 and inevitably headed for better things and life started to run downhill. Aaron wouldn't have had a problem in the world, he thought often, if he had been born white.

But he was the color of rich Turkish coffee, and so he had problems. Most of them stemmed from what was genteelly referred to as "the southern way of life." When the Tars' bus would pull up to cafes in the small towns the club passed through on road trips, Aaron, Mantilla and Garner remained inside, their teammates bringing their food to the bus. "He never said anything, but inside he was seething," a friend said.

There were worse outrages than eating on the bus. On the road, the white players stayed in segregated hotels, the blacks finding their own room and board. "We'd come into town laughing and joking, but when the unloading started at the hotel, everything got quiet," Aaron said. At parks in Montgomery and Savannah and Asheville when the public address announcer would cry "... now batting for Jacksonville, Henry Aaron ..." the silence was deafening. "For more than a month, white people wouldn't applaud us," Aaron remembered, "but finally we won them over."

Not in Montgomery. Not there. Sally League pitchers knocked Henry Aaron down in every city. Why not? There wasn't a more dangerous hitter in the league. But in Montgomery, Aaron would hear cheers when he had to hit the dirt. "People there wrote threatening letters. They'd write they were coming to the park and sit in the right field stands and shoot us. We got all sorts of threats, but it didn't bother me."

A private home in the black section of Jacksonville was Aaron's lone refuge. He was experiencing real racial hatred for the first time. "Playing in the Sally League was a very bad experience for me. 'Jigaboo . . . burr-head.' They called me names I'd never heard of before. Or maybe I'd heard them and they went in one ear and out the other. Maybe I was too dumb as a kid to get mad. I'm not hot-tempered. I wouldn't think about what was said to me from the stands. If I'd gotten those kind of names on the street, it might've been different."

While Aaron was hitting every pitch he could reach, Geraghty was patiently teaching him to play second base, rarely blowing up at the basic mistakes all young players make. When Aaron stole second base three straight times in one game and then was tagged out each time by the second baseman, who had retained the catcher's throws, even Geraghty lost his cool. Aaron accepted the Irishman's tongue-lashings stoically and 20 years later called him "the best manager I ever played for."

Geraghty understood the loneliness that would accrue to young blacks breaking down a major racial barrier. Often he would drop by Aaron's rooming house with a case of Schlitz. "He drank beer and didn't talk about anything but baseball," Aaron said. "But it helped us." Tars' owner Sam Wilson helped, too. Every time Aaron hit a home run, Wilson would tuck an extra $20 in his pay envelope.

But this was 1953 and nightly there were murmurings in the stands about "uppity niggers" and trouble was inevitable. It arrived on a sultry evening in Savannah. Aaron jerked a pitch out of the park and the Savannah pitcher responded according to baseball's finest traditions. "Pickaninny, ain't you a long ways from yo' mama?" he asked Felix Mantilla, before firing a fastball at the shortstop's head. Knocked down by four straight fastballs, Mantilla came out of the dirt screaming epithets at the pitcher and both benches emptied. It was an ugly scene. The bleachers were full of black imaginations fired by pride in Jackie Robinson; the grandstand was equally full of white fears at the impending end of a lifestyle featuring mint juleps on the veranda and darkies in the kitchen. The police were called, tempers flared and Savannah cops carrying submachineguns moved onto the field. "They was getting ready to have a race riot," Aaron said. "More and more policemen came and they announced anyone who came on the field would be shot. I felt bad about it. What happens on the field should be strictly between the players."

Police quieted the situation, the game ended and the Sally League season wore on, Aaron growing more stoic in the face of advancing bigotry. "He got a lot of verbal abuse during the games," said a former teammate. "But I never saw him react to it. He got so he'd come to the clubhouse and never join in the kidding and agitating. He was like a phantom. You never heard him, and away from the park you never saw him."

Aaron retreated into himself, suffering the abuses as Robinson had suffered them a few years before in Brooklyn, unflinchingly and with dignity. "Robinson was my idol," Aaron told a friend. "He gave every black kid in America something to look forward to. He was intelligent, went on about his business and took all the pressure. People talk about the pressure on me, but it's nothing compared to what Jackie went through."

Throughout the long season, Aaron had an ally. She was Barbara Lucas, an 18-year-old business school student he met one spring day at the mailbox outside the Jacksonville ballpark. "She didn't know I was a ballplayer, didn't know who I was," laughed Aaron. They began to date and Aaron spent much of his time away from baseball at the Lucas house, located just a block from the park. "It was like being home, and it settled me down," Aaron said. A self-contained kid out of a Louis Armstrong song, he had momentarily been blinded by the bright lights of Jacksonville. Cutting a swath through Jacksonville after dark, he had done some "experimenting . . . it wasn't hard to find entertainment."

At season's end, the entertainment ceased and Barbara Lucas and Aaron were married. The experimenting didn't end, but took on new form. Aaron was voted the league's MVP after leading the Sally League in six offensive categories including average (.352) and RBIs (125) and finishing second in two others. He was pronounced ready for the majors by the Braves' front office. But not as a second baseman. He had also led the Sally League in another category—errors—and so was to be part of a new type of experiment.

"The way we look at it, you've got too much to learn at second, but you can make it quicker as an outfielder," Braves' farm director John Mullen told Aaron.

Aaron agreed to go to Puerto Rico two days after he was married. Playing the outfield for Caguas of the Puerto Rican Winter League, he was spotted by New York Giant scout Tom Sheehan, who returned to the Giant camp in Phoenix with a prophecy in his mouth.

"Fellas," Sheehan told Giant contemporaries, "I've been feasting my eyes on a kid in the Caribbean who could just turn out to be a better player than Willie Mays. His name is Henry Aaron."

Aaron hit spectacularly in Puerto Rico and became a capable outfielder. With two brilliant minor-league seasons behind him, he was sure all he needed to spend the following year in Milwaukee, where the Braves had moved the previous year, was a break.

4

A Break from Bobby Thomson

There should have been some dramatic celebration of the moment. Trumpets blaring, flags waving, the excited murmurings of shaken multitudes. At the very least, small children tugging anxiously at their fathers' sleeves.

Instead there was silence. One player cursed softly. Another shook his head wearily in resignation. The Braves' equipment man, Joe Taylor, sprinted for second base, where the 1954 Milwaukee season was beginning its death throes. A half-dozen players stood off a way, staring grimly at their teammate huddling in the dust, his right leg grotesquely bent. Someone said "get a stretcher." With no more fanfare than that, the season was carried from the field.

It had been a routine play, the boring stuff of a thousand exhibition games. The ball squirted deep into the left-field corner and reappeared in the sunlight, darting up the cinder warning track that ran parallel with the outfield wall.

Rookie Hank gets handshake from manager Charlie Grimm as he rounds third following spring training home run in 1954.

Bobby Thomson turned first with the ease of a sea-soned veteran and dug hard for second. The leftfielder's throw came on a line, low and true. Thomson fell away from the tag like a feather, but the spikes on his right shoe jammed deep into a rut on the baseline. The bone in his right leg, just above the ankle, broke neatly, a triple fracture. Thomson bit his lower lip against the pain, while in the dugout runway a young man named Henry Aaron stood idly drinking a Coke, unaware that fate was reaching out for him.

Sometimes it happens that way. Seasons end before they have ever begun. A Wilt Chamberlain or a Jimmy Brown or a Bobby Orr makes moves they have made countless times. Only this time something snaps or tears or breaks, and the pain is felt by dozens of others.

So it was in the case of Bobby Thomson, come to Milwaukee in saviour's clothing to provide leadership and a big bat, or perhaps even the sort of miracle he had wrought three years before for the New York Giants.

Even now, 23 years later, the memory of Bobby Thomson forms a small ice ball in the pit of the stomach of every baseball fan over 30, worthy of that designation.

Bobby Thomson. The Giants coming like the tide in the stretch of the 1951 season. Inexorably. Gathering to their breasts an enthralled nation caught up in their fiery pursuit of the impossible dream. And then at the apex of that dream, a crisp fall afternoon in New York . . . Dodger pitching coach Clyde Sukeforth ignoring Clem Labine's wickedly twisting curveball, enamored of the steadiness of Ralph Branca . . . Sukeforth picking up the bullpen telephone and advising manager Charlie Dressen to let the season ride with Branca . . . Andy Pafko running out of room, desperately pressing his shoulderblades against the left-field fence at the Polo Grounds . . . and the ball disappearing, far beyond his reach. The Miracle of Coogan's

Bluff complete. An event that made men's eyes go wet and women scream. The single most delirious moment in baseball history; unfettered delight; Giant manager Leo Durocher berserk with excitement and joy and absolution, his red face an uplifted index finger to the rest of baseball. Bobby Thomson. The Giants resurrected from the July grave from which they had scrambled, one painful rung after another, to force a playoff with the mighty Dodgers, the nation's desire for such a miracle growing game by game. Bobby Thomson. His blast, high and deep into the blue autumnal sky off a Branca curveball that had hung there as inviting as a rose. Until then, baseball's most memorable home run.

Three years later, on a fine spring day in Bradenton, Florida, he was wearing the uniform of the Milwaukee Braves, who if they did not expect quite so magnificent a miracle from Thomson, nevertheless counted him as holding the key to the 1954 season.

So respected as a power hitter and defensive outfielder was Thomson that during the winter the Braves had parted with four players and $50,000 to acquire his services. Gone to New York for Thomson were onetime $100,000 bonus boy Johnny Antonelli, a pitcher of vast promise; stylish lefty Don Liddle; Ebba St. Claire, a catcher who ran to fat and soon ate himself out of the game; and infielder Bobby Klaus, who would stay afloat in the majors a dozen more years. Such was the value the Braves placed on Thomson.

They had won 92 games in 1953, but defensive leaks in left field and at second base had proved ruinous and the Braves finished no less than 13 games behind pennant-winning Brooklyn. Clearly changes were necessary and the Braves decided on two: one, to replace heavy-legged Sid Gordon in left, and a second deal which brought Danny O'Connell's slick glove from Pittsburgh to unseat the defensively inadequate Jack Dittmar at second base.

But the Braves' 1954 season was to focus on Thomson, and days after training camp opened, he slid into second base and didn't arise. Fate was pointing to a lightly-schooled outfielder named Henry Aaron, who had stood unconcernedly watching Thomson carried from the field, unaware that his career had just lurched upward. "Hell, I wasn't mature enough to realize anything more than sunup, sundown and mealtime. I certainly didn't know that when they carried Thomson by me on the way to the hospital that was my ticket to the majors.

Searching for a replacement, Braves' manager Charlie Grimm had several possibilities. A third-year pro named Jim Pendleton was the top choice. But there were other possibilities: Dick Sinovic had hit .342 for Atlanta in the Southern Association; a flake named Pete Whisenant hit with power and was a capable defensive player; a Brave reserve, Bob Thorpe; and George Metkovich, who had been with two other National League clubs and was clinging in the big leagues by his fingertips. Oh, yeah, and a reputed phenom named Aaron who had just been converted from second base and was ticketed to go to Toledo in the American Association.

Grimm figured he might as well find out about the unknown quantity quickly—"I didn't believe anyone could be as good as I heard he was"—and the next day moved Aaron into Thomson's spot in an exhibition against Cincinnati. Aaron singled, tripled and hit a tremendous home run.

Grimm chuckled to himself watching the ball still rising as it left the Tampa park. Days earlier the equipment man, Joe Taylor, had come to his office and told Grimm "there's a skinny, colored kid in the clubhouse carrying a duffle bag."

"When I saw him, I thought he had come to deliver a telegram," Grimm laughed later. "But it didn't take long to know he was something special. He hit Warren Spahn's screwballs and curves all over the place. Some of my coaches didn't like the way he batted, kind of unorthodox, but I told them, 'The way he hits, it would be a shame to fool with him.' "

As the spring exhibition grind rolled on, Aaron remained in the competition for Thomson's job, becoming increasingly confident he could hold it. "I was ready. I hit good in Puerto Rico and I kept it up." In Sarasota one afternoon, Ted Williams was talking to a teammate during an exhibition game with Milwaukee. Suddenly, Williams was jolted from the conversation by the ringing sound of a bat meeting a ball.

"Who the hell hit that one?" Williams asked.

"Aaron, a new kid," replied a Milwaukee writer.

"Sounds like a hell of a hitter."

Aaron was. He had improved significantly over the winter while playing in Puerto Rico for former Brooklyn catcher Mickey Owen, a stickler for hitting the ball to all fields. Before going to Puerto Rico, Aaron had been primarily a pull hitter, perhaps unconsciously swayed by Tommy Holmes' rebuke that he would never make the major leagues unless he took full advantage of his power. Owens insisted that as a rookie Aaron would be uncovered as a fast-ball hitter and then be fed a steady diet of outside breaking pitches. "You've got to learn to hit the ball to right, too," Owens said, ordering Aaron to hit two balls to left field and three to right during batting practice. "I got used to doing that and after a while it just came naturally to do it in games," Aaron said.

Other things did not come so naturally. At Caguas, Aaron was being converted into an outfielder, a move which pleased him. "When I played second base at Jacksonville, I was afraid of runners coming in. That's the hardest position on the field. The runners come in and you've got your back to them. Anything can happen."

Anything could happen when Aaron went to the plate, too. He was undisciplined, giving thought to nothing but the duel between himself and the pitcher. The year before at Jacksonville, manager Ben Geraghty had given him the take sign and Aaron had ignored it, driving the ball from the premises.

"Why didn't you take that pitch?" Geraghty demanded.

"I thought it was the hit sign."

"That was the *old* hit sign."

"Heck, Ben, I just learned that one the other day."

At the Braves' camp, all attempts to alter his running style—shuffling stiff-legged on his heels—failed. When asked why he didn't try to sprint, Aaron told a Braves' coach, "I'm pacin' myself."

But as it had with the Clowns and in the minor leagues, Aaron's bat was eloquent and just compensation for a lack of polish. He continued to hit through the spring and said little to anyone. "If I spoke three words, it was an upset. I just wasn't any kind of talker."

Before long he had attracted the notice of the Braves' regulars, who were fretful over Thomson's replacement. "I didn't remember him at first," said Eddie Mathews, the club's biggest stick. "And there was no reason why I should have. Regulars don't pay much attention to rookies and he wasn't even on our roster. I'd heard there was a kid second-baseman at Jacksonville that supposedly was a cinch to make it big, but you hear that stuff all the time. It was the Bobby Thomson crackup that made me aware of Aaron."

Aaron was aware, however, of Mathews. "I was even a little awed by him. He was the home run champion of the National League and I was only a rookie. I didn't even introduce myself to him."

Few introductions were needed after the Braves saw

61

Aaron swing the bat, and a few days before Milwaukee broke camp and headed north, Grimm called the rookie aside.

"Kid, you're my leftfielder. It's yours until someone takes it away from you," he said.

A classic case of the gnarled old manager putting his chips on the untested rookie? Hollywood has a million spinoffs on that basic theme. But Henry Aaron thought it was a phony. "I'd read stories about players being told that and then winding up playing left bar stool in Saginaw, Michigan."

Aaron's cynicism was, however, unfounded. On opening day of the 1954 season, the Brave outfield showed Andy Pafko in right, Billy Bruton in center, and in left, the kid from Mobile, Henry Aaron.

"All the breaks came my way that spring," Aaron said. "Including the one to Thomson's leg. That opened it up for me." Jim Pendleton clinched it. He had come to camp an odds-on choice to be the Braves' fourth outfielder, a multi-talented player with speed and power. And a gut. While Aaron was remaining in shape, hitting .326 and dominating the Puerto Rican winter league in the power departments, Pendleton was succumbing to *la dolce vita* and reported to Bradenton far overweight. When Pendleton failed to make it, Aaron learned a valuable lesson. "Big Jim was too heavy and Charlie Grimm got mad at him and gave me the job. Never let a manager get mad at you."

The day before the season began, Brave general manager John Quinn signed Aaron to a Milwaukee contract and on opening day in Cincinnati, he hit a home run off Vic Raschi, the old Yankee fireballer. "Nobody on our team knew anything about Aaron except our manager, Eddie Stanky," Raschi said. "He knew Aaron was potentially a great ballplayer and he talked about everything except the way he parted his hair. He had such great wrists, and it was hard to fool him." Raschi had precious little luck doing that, also giving up the last of the 13 home runs Aaron hit his rookie year.

During that first year Aaron impressed some observers, left others wondering if there would be consistency to his performance and his blandness, which the press strived mightily to gloss over. But as a baseball player, he was pure talent, according to the best judges, his peers.

As a hitter, they held precious few doubts about Aaron. Said the man fast becoming his confidant on the club, Billy Bruton, "The first time I saw him hit a home run, the shortstop leaped for the ball, thinking he could catch it." A spectator most of 1954, Bobby Thomson admitted his earliest skepticism was unfounded. "Magic is the only way to describe it," he said of Aaron at the bat. "You had this feeling even then but this guy was something special. He was far removed from the ordinary class of ballplayer like the rest of us. Everybody had said he was bound to be a great one, but nobody really gave him much thought. He'd hit well in the minors, sure, but we figured he'd be like so many rookies before him—come to camp with a big reputation, really see the curveball for the first time, and bomb out."

Aaron had no idea of bombing out. "I kept reading the Braves had lost the pennant when Bobby Thomson broke his leg. That didn't do my confidence any good, but I was still a silent kid. I didn't want to say anything that was going to open the trap door and I'd find myself on the way to Toledo."

Early in the 1954 season, even after an eight-game exhibition swing with Brooklyn during which he had hit .407, Aaron had his detractors. But his hero, Jackie Robinson, scoffed at them. "On what he's shown against us, he's ready," Robinson said. "He hit our pitching good;

sure, he runs on his heels, but he gets around the bases and covers a lot of ground. Who could ask for anything more?"

Aaron's Puerto Rico tutor, Mickey Owen, agreed. "He has an outfielder's arm and he's smart. He won't make the same mistake twice." Aaron also had some champions among the Braves. "He's going to peel some pitcher off the mound some day," predicted the hulking first baseman, Joe Adcock. "Everything the kid hits is a line drive. And he hits more line drives through the box than anyone I ever saw."

In April and May, Aaron made about as many mental errors as anyone had ever seen. One day his hat blew off and he went back to retrieve it, subsequently failing to score when an outfielder booted the ball. The next day he stood rooted between second and third base watching a long fly ball and had to flee back to second when the ball was caught rather than advancing a base. But these were the garish, understandable errors of inexperience. "He was very quiet, all eyes," remembered the Braves' fiery shortstop, Johnny Logan. "He was a line-drive hitter but he fell in with Eddie Mathews and Adcock and said, 'Hmmmm, I can hit with these guys.' Then it seemed that every time Eddie hit a home run, Hank followed with another in that game or the next one."

Despite Aaron's steadiness at the plate and afield—he fought no serious slumps and committed only seven errors—the Milwaukee Braves of 1954 resembled nothing so much as a kite in an inconsistent breeze. They faltered early, surged briefly, faltered again. But none of the eight teams in the National League was in a mood to take charge of the pennant race, and in a six-day stretch in late May, no less than four clubs held first place briefly.

Certainly Aaron had his problems with major-league pitching. No pitch was safe from his ambition. "I make up my mind to swing, I swing. I don't look for no walks."

When he developed a reputation as a notorious bad-ball hitter, pitchers were quick to exploit it. On one memorable occasion, he lunged wildly and drilled a pitch over the right-field fence in Milwaukee—and was promptly called out for having stepped out of the batter's box.

Susceptible to off-speed breaking pitches, Aaron saw little else in the summer of 1954, but he quickly adapted. "I disciplined myself to wait for the good pitch. I eventually get them, but I have to be patient."

Patience became a virtue for both the Braves and Aaron. The New York Giants, with Johnny Antonelli winning the clutch games, finally took command of the National League pennant race, and on July 22nd led Brooklyn by 7½ games and the Braves by 15, only to have Milwaukee shake another slump and come roaring back.

Aaron, Eddie Mathews and Joe Adcock led the resurgence, the Braves winning 20 of their next 22 games to pull the Giants back to within a half game of Brooklyn and 3½ of Milwaukee. "They started getting me out on change-ups," Aaron said. "So I started waiting for them, even letting a good fastball go by. Pretty soon I'd learned to hit the change-up good, so they stopped throwing them."

The Braves made the final run at the Giants around Labor Day, inching up to within four games of front-running New York going into a crucial two-game series in Brooklyn. They lost both games, the first one a five-inning rain-plagued affair during which the umpires waited two hours before calling the game with the Brooks up, 2–1.

For Henry Aaron, however, the 1954 season had ended two days before Labor Day, ironically in the same manner Bobby Thomson's year had ended even before it began. With the Braves only five games behind New York, Henry Aaron had five straight hits as Milwaukee was sweeping a doubleheader in Cincinnati. The last hit was a triple, but Aaron stumbled sliding into third base and his right ankle snapped. Irony stepped into the picture as they were taking Aaron to the hospital. Bobby Thomson, who had returned to the lineup in August, came in to run for him.

A pin was placed in Aaron's ankle—after doctors got permission to operate from Estella Aaron, who at first had balked by hollering into the phone, "don't you go cutting on my boy." The operation was a success, and proved to be, well, a break for Aaron. The following year he was declared ineligible for the draft because of the steel pin in his leg.

For Aaron, in most ways his rookie season had been satisfying. He hit .280, and only 27 National League batters bettered that mark. His 13 home runs included at least one in each park in the league. He got on well with manager Charlie Grimm, who only criticized him privately, something Aaron would long remember. "If he had bawled me out in front of all those veterans we had at the time, there's no telling what would've happened to me, because in your first year you're scared all the time anyway."

Others knew fear, too. The Braves' publicity man, an iconoclastic three-and-a-half foot tall midget named Don Davidson, had nicknamed Aaron "Hank" in an attempt to enliven the image of the sloe-eyed rookie. Reporters had lengthened that *nom de guerre* to "Hammerin' Hank." But the Brooklyn pitching staff, witnessing the birth of a player who would surely become a hitter of stature, had another name for Aaron. Dodger pitchers called him Bad Henry.

"We used to go over the opposing lineup and nobody ever wanted to pitch to him," said Dodger pitching coach Preston Gomez, now the manager of the Houston Astros.

"Soon all of the guys were calling him Bad Henry and the name spread around the league."

Aaron, however, was edged out in the voting for the Rookie of the Year by St. Louis Cardinal outfielder Wally Moon, who had hit .304 in 148 games. There was some indication the Baseball Writers of America had been unduly influenced by the fact that in the seven previous seasons, Alvin Dark had been the only white player to receive the award. But Aaron was not bitter.

"I was disappointed at not winning," he said, "but not because Moon didn't deserve it. He did. I just thought I could've done better."

Next year, and in the years to come, Bad Henry would do exactly that.

5

"Is That Really Robin Roberts?"

Spring training. Lovely, warm, cloudless days. The greening of baseball. Pulled hamstrings, and young phenoms wide-eyed at their first real look at the slider, and managers who talk about running more and bunting more and, by God, making curfew more.

Spring training. Kid smoke-throwers who can't find the plate and worn-out junkballers who, to survive, must. Flaming youth and burned-out age. St. Pete and Scottsdale and Tampa, and exhibitions that don't mean a damn to the few who have it made and everything to the many who don't. Spring training. When every team is a winner.

Spring training, 1955. Under the brilliant Florida sun, the Milwaukee Braves were learning how to become winners. It would take another manager and time and a crushing disappointment and the blooming of one young man before they were to put their hands on a pennant, but on this mid-March afternoon they were pursuing their grail. In two years, the team, and Henry Aaron, would acquire the maturity necessary to uncovering it.

The pitchers, and the catchers necessary to their art, are the advance men of spring training. When the remainder of the team arrives, they own an advantage, and on March 23, 1956, a strong-armed, confident nameless young man was firing fastball after fastball past bats laden with winter rust.

Henry Aaron stepped into the cage, swung the bat lazily and squared his weight on both feet, digging the right one hard into the dirt in search of a foothold. Comfortable now, he nodded toward the mound. The kid pitcher threw his fastball. Henry Aaron drove it on an even line over the centerfield fence of the Bradenton ballpark. The kid threw again. A second drive cleared the fence in almost the same spot. A third straight fastball went the way of the other two.

Aaron grinned. "Ol' Henry is ready."

"Youth is a great thing," Braves' manager Charlie Grimm laughed in the dugout, watching Aaron overpower the ball. "Look at that kid go. You'd never know he broke his ankle six months ago."

Throughout 1955, as it became apparent Milwaukee needed a little more pitching and a little more defense and maybe a tad more speed to compete with the Dodgers, who were in the golden years of Brooklyn baseball, it also became apparent that Henry Aaron was making the transition from good major leaguer to great major leaguer.

If the news media had portrayed him as a dullard—and it had—his bat gave lie to any such thoughts. Having failed at luring him into incompetence with the change-up, National League pitchers switched tactics early in 1955, as the Dodgers were making a mockery of the pennant chase.

"They stopped throwing the change-up and went with

A day of joy for the Braves, victorious over the New York Giants as, left to right, Bobby Thomson, Gene Conley, Danny O'Connell and Hank Aaron led the way in April, 1955.

the outside pitch," Aaron said. "I went with them and started to hit the ball to right. I guess that discouraged 'em."

Something surely did. Aaron was the picture of consistency in the first few months of the season, but the Braves could not muster any sort of challenge to the Dodgers. Brooklyn, which had opened the season with 10 straight wins, won 10 of 11 games in the first two weeks of June to take an 11½-game lead over the Braves and stretch its won-lost record to a convincing 58–26.

The good burghers of Milwaukee took a realistic view of the situation and continued to turn out at County Stadium in record numbers, mostly to empathize with the hugely agreeable Grimm and cheer the hugely talented Aaron.

In fact, Aaron was Grimm's only solace. The Braves had undergone a series of ruinous injuries. Lanky Gene Conley won 11 of his first 16 decisions before developing a shoulder ailment that sidelined him the rest of the season. Joe Adcock's booming bat was silenced for good in August when he was hit on the wrist by a pitch. Eddie Mathews was the league home run king until he had to have an appendectomy. Overworked, Warren Spahn tailed off badly and was just a shade better than a .500 pitcher. There was talk Grimm's job was hanging by the proverbial thread.

Through it all, Henry Aaron strode onward and upward. In June, he was leading the league with a .322 average and was picked to the all-star team by manager Leo Durocher. Aaron replaced the Giants' Don Mueller in the fifth inning and had two hits and a walk, and drove in the tying run that enabled Stan Musial to win the game for the National League with a 12th-inning home run.

Still, Aaron was dissatisfied, as he had been with his rookie performance. Told Ty Cobb (.240), Rogers

Hornsby (.246) and Willie Mays (.274) had not matched him in their first years, Aaron shrugged. "That still don't make me feel better that I didn't hit but two-eighty."

Now, in July of only his second season, he had 22 home runs and a .325 average, and still he drove himself. "Those runs-batted-in . . . that's what I'm aiming for. They seem more important than your batting average. When you have a lot of RBIs, you know you're doing something for your team."

What Aaron did could have no major effect on Milwaukee, and although he finished his second season with a .314 average, 27 home runs, and a team-leading 106 RBIs, the Braves finished a distant second to Brooklyn, which won its third pennant in four years by 13½ games.

New York finished third, thanks in some measure to Aaron, who ripped Giant pitching for five home runs, 22 RBIs and a .398 average. He was named Milwaukee's Player of the Year, an award that gave Charlie Grimm pause to reflect on an earlier statement.

"I've said in the past that Henry wouldn't go as far as Willie Mays—but it could be I am mistaken," observed Grimm. "I think he's going to be a better hitter than Mays and he's almost as good a fielder right now."

His average and runs output dramatically improved, a proven hitter and confident now, Aaron sought to increase his home run production. "I'll be in there workin' on it," he told a reporter at the close of the 1955 season. "I ain't scared any more."

Mathews, the white Brave with whom Aaron was closest, had no doubts he would soon have a serious challenger on his own club for the league home run leadership. "It was probably the middle of the 1955 season before I realized Henry was a home run hitter," Mathews said. "His power was to right and right center. That means he'll hit more homers as he grows older and learns to pull the ball more."

Aaron spent the winter fishing and loafing and playing with daughter Gaile, born the previous summer. The Braves' front office spent the winter searching for reasons why a club which had power from Mathews, Adcock and Aaron; which had three fine starters in Spahn, Lou Burdette and Bob Buhl; which had an adequate bullpen and was defensively strong up the middle, was not winning nor even challenging for the pennant.

Charlie Grimm seemed to be part of the answer and when spring training began in 1956, he was a marked man, something which did not particularly please Aaron, who had enjoyed an amicable relationship with the manager.

One day that spring, Grimm smiled toward Aaron and told a writer, "There's the guy that's liable to be leading the league in hitting this season, and several seasons after this one."

It was an excellent prophecy, but Grimm was not around to see it fulfilled. Early in the season the Braves continued to manifest the streakiness which had become their trademark. They could not get themselves untracked and enmity grew between Grimm and his boss, general manager John Quinn.

In May, Quinn called a clubhouse meeting and heatedly lectured the Braves for a lack of hustle, striding from the room angrily. Grimm stood up and defended his players. "I know you're hustling . . . so hard that you're pressing." After losing the opening two games of a series in Brooklyn on June 17th, the Braves owned a 24–22 record and Quinn fired Grimm, replacing him with small, tough Fred Haney, fresh from two disastrous seasons with the inept Pittsburgh Pirates.

As often occurs after a change of leadership, the Braves immediately turned the season around, winning 12 straight games. Aaron had not gotten involved in the firing of Grimm, which was naturally a popular source of club-house debate. "What do you think about Charlie?" short-stop Johnny Logan had asked. "I don't think," Aaron replied. "I just come here to hit."

Early in Haney's reign, Milwaukee took 15 of 17 to climb over Brooklyn and into first place. Aaron did not accept Haney as he had the genial Grimm, but it wasn't reflected in his performance.

The breadth of Aaron's strike zone—once laughingly described by Grimm as "a general area ranging from the top of his head to the tips of his toes"—continued to baffle National League pitchers.

"I've seen him hit pitches right off his ear into the right field grandstand," moaned Pittsburgh's Bob Friend. Said another hurler, "The last two pitches I threw at his head, he hit out of the park."

Aaron was not moved to delve deeply into his skills. "I just keep swinging," he said, leading the league in hitting in mid-August. "I have no trouble seeing the ball. The only time I get in trouble is when my timing is off. Then I hit nothing."

Haney had a theory concerning why a third-year hitter was dominating the averages and ranking in the top five in the power departments. "He's relaxed, ready, and you don't have to worry about him passing up a good pitch," Haney said. "He's as fine a natural hitter as I've come across."

Aaron agreed he was only doing what came naturally. "Leastwise, that's what everyone says," he smiled. "I never took a hitting lesson in my life. I just can't wait until my turn to hit comes up again."

Throughout the raging race between the Braves, the Dodgers, the Giants and Cincinnati, there were stretches when Aaron carried Milwaukee. He hit safely in 25 straight games in midsummer before being blanked by the Cards' Herm Wehmeier, who said: "I was lucky. Once last year, I threw him one low and inside. You know where he hit it? In the upper right field bleachers."

Applying the lash that Grimm had eschewed, Haney had the Braves atop the National League standings no less than 126 days. He was harsh and would accept nothing less than aggressive baseball.

When the Braves threatened to fall into their old habit of inconsistency—and in 1956 they did it enough for Aaron to describe them as "twenty-five guys on a see-saw"—Haney was hard to please.

"One day in New York I hit a ball pretty hard at the shortstop and Mr. Haney claimed I hadn't run the ball out," said Aaron, who would be accused of that sin throughout his career. "But I'd given it the best I knew how."

Haney grated on his players even as the Braves held first place and his criticism rankled Aaron, who took his complaint to the team captain, catcher Del Crandall.

"I told Crandall that if this guy [Haney] wants me to play for him, he better stay off my back. So Crandall went to him and told him about it, and Haney never did say anything else to me."

In the hard, hot days of late August, the Braves began to slip, and on Sept. 11 against the Dodgers, Sal Maglie outpitched Bob Buhl and Brooklyn took over the lead. The two teams, with Cincinnati breathing hot on them, came down the stretch together, and the Braves finally withered under the pressure, although Aaron did not.

Adcock and Mathews fell into slumps around Labor Day, and suddenly Burdette and Buhl couldn't get anyone out, winning only three games between them the rest of the year.

The 1956 pennant race narrowed to the wire with the Braves clinging to a one-game lead with three games to play. Milwaukee was at St. Louis; the Dodgers were hosting the lowly Pirates. When the Braves dropped their first two games with the Cardinals while Brooklyn was twice steamrollering Pittsburgh, it was all over. Burdette had the best earned-run average in the league and the most shutouts; Spahn's 20 wins were a league-high and he was the runnerup in ERA; Adcock had tied for home run honors with 38 and Mathews added 37. Only two clubs in the NL had committed fewer errors. Aaron hit .328 and also led the league in hits (200), total bases (340) and doubles (34). And still it hadn't been enough. The Braves trailed pennant-winning Brooklyn by one game. And Fred Haney was livid.

"Go home and get a good rest, a very good rest," he told the Braves after the final game. "Get rested . . . because when you go to Bradenton, you're going to have a hell of a spring."

They were the team of the future and they had the *player* of the future, and Fred Haney was going to win a pennant in 1957. Aaron was looking forward to just that. "I should hit 15 points better next year," he said, after winning his first batting title with a .328 average. "I know the pitchers better and I have lots more confidence now."

Aaron, indeed, was confident. He was many things more complex than the public knew or was to become aware of for many years. But after three seasons in the majors—partly because of his placid personality and a truly sardonic sense of humor, and partly because few reporters had the patience or industriousness to interview him at any length—Henry Aaron was painted publicly as a rather simple-minded young man. It was generally accepted that he was a quiet colored boy possessed of a singular skill. And, because Charlie Grimm and several other people in the Brave organization had pixyish ideas on giving Aaron some color, he was viewed in some quarters as a semi-flake.

"I've read some newspapermen saying I was just a dumb kid from the south with no education and that all I knew was to go out there and hit. They didn't know how to talk to me; then wrote I didn't know how to talk to them. Newspapermen build up a lot of stories, and they built them up about me. I got wise to them, but what could I do?"

So came about the collection of Hank Aaron "stories," most of them rather unfunny works of fiction. There was the Robin Roberts Story, which was true, and the Ford Frick Telegram Caper, which wasn't. And soon Aaron saw himself pictured as Young Stepin Fetchit, a comforting thought to the white baseball fan, perhaps, but a cruel caricature which Aaron bitterly resented but bore, as he did all things, without a whimper. Individually, the Aaron stories, many of them wholly from the inventive mind of Grimm, were harmless; collectively they were something else.

Certainly as a young player Aaron was lacking in sophistication, but he was no more ignorant than any 20-year-old has a right to be. Robin Roberts may have been the darling of baseball in general and Philadelphia in particular, but he wasn't exactly a household word in Toulminville. One day in 1956 Aaron hit a long home run off a Roberts fastball and when a teammate remarked, "I hope you realize you just hit that off the best pitcher in baseball," Aaron's innate honesty asserted itself. "Not to me, he ain't," Aaron smiled. After the quote became public—he supposedly said with a wide-eyed look, "is that really Robin Roberts?"—Aaron had difficulty hitting the veteran righthander as long as he remained in baseball.

Aaron's reputation for clownish ignorance came indirectly from Grimm. In 1955, several Braves began spring training workouts ahead of the date established by the National League office and were routinely fined for the infraction by Commissioner Ford Frick. They were informed of the cursory fine by telegram. Aaron glanced at it, tossed it in his locker, and promptly forgot about it. Later, Grimm asked to see it and Aaron couldn't recall where he had put it. "Someone, probably Charlie Grimm, told the newspapers I had thrown it in the wastebasket. That's how wrong impressions are made. Some people *wanted* to think I was dumb—because I was a Negro."

Asked how Aaron liked flying, the Braves' traveling secretary told reporters, "No one knows; he's asleep before the plane leaves the ground." Said Aaron, "I didn't know who he was talking about. Sure, I slept on trips, but not until I was sure the pilot had gotten us off the ground, and even then I had one eye open."

The late *New York Times* sports columnist Arthur Daley once described a checker game in which Aaron, supposedly asleep, was shaken awake and immediately reached over and made a triple jump. "He relaxes in sleepy-eyed languor," wrote Daley, whose capture of a Pulitzer Prize remains a continuing source of amusement to his contemporaries.

Still, Aaron's occasional gaffe contributed to his image. Asked if he preferred the outfield to second base, he replied, "I sure do. There's not as much to do and I don't like hard work."

Lost in the maze of nonsensical or untrue anecdotes was Aaron's wry sense of humor. His virtues paraded excessively by Braves' owner Lou Perini one night at a baseball writers banquet, Aaron nudged his buddy Billy Bruton and yawned, "Does he mean all that before I sign my contract or after?" Months later Aaron, who had filled in briefly at second base when Danny O'Connell had fallen into a deep slump, returned his unsigned contract to general manager John Quinn along with a note that inquired if Quinn had "sent me O'Connell's contract by mistake?"

Aaron was, and is, a private person. His beliefs do not

surface easily in conversation and in his early years in baseball, few reporters probed with any particular insight into his character.

His honest statements—asked his biggest thrill in the game, he told a reporter it had come when making the final putout to nail down a no-hitter for Jim Wilson during the 1954 season—were interpreted as platitudes.

"I can't recall when any writer has spent enough time with me to write a sensible story," he said, excluding the beat men who covered the Braves daily. But even they had nothing more than a pedestrian understanding of Aaron's psyche.

If he was not a man of huge intellectual appetites, neither was he Stepin Fetchit, the bug-eyed, idiot darky stereotype white America was forced to abandon in the mid-1950s.

"I take life seriously—always did—but I'm not aloof," Aaron protested his image. "I don't hide from anyone."

In 1956, however, an image had been created and it would not be dissolved for years to come. He was sleepy-eyed, quiet, old Henry Aaron, who hit flat spots on baseballs and had a personality to match. Certainly the former was true, and never would it be truer than in 1957.

Hank Aaron and Ed Mathews couldn't know in 1957 that fate would link them on a special day in 1974.

6

"I Just Want To Be Known As A Singles Hitter"

He is older now; going to fat. He takes longer between pitches, deep breaths jiggling heavy jowls. Hitters he used to overpower, he now laboriously sets up for the curveball. He has outlived the Roes and Erskines and Blacks of the Dodgers' glory years, but his guile and the curve and his heart are still intact, and he is still one of the good ones.

On this warm spring afternoon in 1957, he stands on the mound studying the slender hitter slowly making his way to the plate. In the second inning, Don Newcombe started Henry Aaron out with an inside fastball. Aaron pulled it into the left-center power alley for a double. Three innings later, Big Newk had fed Aaron an off-speed slider. The ball had come blazing back through the box, narrowly missing the big pitcher, and had been caught by the Dodger centerfielder a foot from the ground.

He'll be guessing, Newcombe knew. The good ones always do. Twice Aaron guessed wrong, fouling off a pitch, taking another on the corner for a called strike. The third pitch was automatic coming from an experienced pitcher. Waste it low and away. Newcombe did. Aaron golfed it to right-center and coasted into second with another double.

Newcombe strode purposefully toward second base, his broad face twisted by frustration. "Next time," he shouted at Aaron, "I'm going to throw the damn thing *under* the plate. See can you hit *that*."

Brushing the dirt from his uniform, Henry Aaron chuckled. If he had reached the day when he could unnerve Big Newk, he had indeed arrived as a major league hitter of import.

And Henry Aaron had arrived by early in 1957, although one day during spring training he had blithely informed a reporter, "I just want to be known as a singles hitter."

True to his word, Brave manager Fred Haney had assumed the role of Legree during spring training. "Mistakes" would halt practice and the entire Brave troupe would take a lap around the field. A home run was a mistake; an error was a mistake; a mental lapse was a mistake. Being late on the field was a mistake. The Braves thrived on a diet of Haney's lash, however.

"We were there to practice being perfect," Aaron said. "I don't think I ever saw a team open a season as determined to win the pennant."

At first blush, the Braves played as though intent on winning it before May 15th. They broke on top, taking 10 of their first 11 games, but the 1957 pennant race was to go down as one of the meanest, most desperate in baseball history.

The Braves entered the fray well prepared, Haney tongue-lashing his troops from the opening bell at training camp. He was de-fused only once that spring. When Aaron had reported a day late, Haney braced him.

"Why are you late?" he asked.

"I was late catching the train from Mobile."

"Why didn't you start out sooner?"

"Then I would have reported here too soon."

Haney dropped the subject. He had already gotten no better than a draw in one meeting of the minds with Aaron. Having reprimanded Aaron publicly the year before, Haney had earned the player's enmity. "If you want to scold me, fine, take me in private and do it," Aaron told the feisty Haney. "But don't do it out in the open."

A truce in force, Aaron triggered the Braves to a quick start and before long a trade had turned him into the Milwaukee cleanup man. Hanging in the middle of a five-team chase that also included St. Louis, Cincinnati, Brooklyn, and Philadelphia, the Milwaukee front office took a calculated gamble and pulled off a major deal just before the June 15th trading deadline. The irrepressible Danny O'Connell had been inconsistent at both the plate and afield, and general manager John Quinn decided a change was in order. Consequently, he shipped O'Connell, the aging Bobby Thomson (hitting .150 at the time), and pitcher Ray Crone to the New York Giants for a man to fill the bill at second, Red Schoendienst.

Schoendienst steadied the Brave infield and Aaron continued to hammer National League pitching, but on July 29 only 2½ games separated the first five teams in the National League. And the importance of Henry Aaron to the Braves' acquiring their first pennant in Milwaukee had become increasingly well understood. When Milwaukee slumped briefly in July, Milwaukee *Sentinel* baseball writer Red Thisted observed, "It's a little unfair to Aaron, but it may as well be admitted now that when he isn't swishing that bat with authority, the Braves are in trouble."

The writer's comment pleased Aaron. "It told me that people were expecting me to be the leader. If you're going to be the big man on your ball club, you've got to be able to carry the load. That was the first time I ever saw anything that said, in effect, 'As Aaron goes, so go the Braves.' "

Indeed, by late July, Aaron was going well and so were the Braves. So well was Aaron hitting—his .348 average, 28 home runs and 75 RBIs were high in the major leagues —that he was the talk of baseball.

"He's the most unpredictable hitter in the game," said Brooklyn catcher Roy Campanella, who might have been talking about himself. "He has less strikes on him than any guy in the league. He don't go up takin'." Watching Aaron tear up the National League from close range, teammate Wes Covington said, "He's the most unemotional ballplayer I've ever seen. Home runs or outs, he comes back to the dugout with the same disposition. If he goes 0-for-3, he'll say 'I'm going to get me something tomorrow.' And chances are he'll get five hits the next day.

Thought Philadelphia manager Mayo Smith: "There's no book on him. You have to pitch him like you do Yogi Berra—right down the middle with everything you've got on it and then close your eyes."

After a Milwaukee tear, that began August 10th and had eliminated all but the Cardinals as a contender when it was spent 19 games and 17 wins later, Fred Haney was driven to superlatives.

"Aaron is more like Hornsby than any hitter I ever saw," he enthused. "And Rogers Hornsby was the greatest righthanded hitter I ever saw. It is incredible the way that kid can hit the ball to right with all that power. And he's more than just a natural hitter. He has the temperament and disposition to go with it."

Aaron saw no great mystery in a bid to win the triple crown. "I always hit the ball where it's pitched," he said.

"I try to learn what a pitcher's best pitch is, and then when he's in trouble, I look for him to use it."

Late in the summer of 1957, Aaron had a new indication of the respect his bat was commanding. Pitchers had decided when in trouble to simply throw at Aaron, rather than to him. And no one threw at Aaron harder or closer than a brash young Dodger, Don Drysdale.

Twice he knocked Aaron down in a game in August and afterward a misquote brought Aaron grief. "Somebody quoted me saying 'it didn't bother me. That punk doesn't throw hard enough to bother me.' I never said that."

Weeks later, after being knocked down continuously in a series in St. Louis, Aaron breeched baseball's unwritten law.

"Sam Jones and Larry Jackson were throwing at me like I was a target in one of those carnival booths," he said. "Finally, I had enough. I told a reporter, 'I'm going out there and get me one of those gentlemen the next time they throw at me.' "

Joe Adcock, who had broken a leg in June and wouldn't be back in uniform until September, called Aaron aside. "The worst thing you can do is start jawing about it," Adcock said. "All you're doing is inviting more of it. Do whatever you feel like doing, but don't talk about it in the newspapers."

Gradually, Aaron convinced National League pitchers that a head-high fastball was no antidote for his potent bat. "You can afford to lose some teeth, you bastard," Johnny Antonelli snarled at him one day after he had jerked an Antonelli pitch off the left-field wall for a double. "But can *you*?" Aaron chuckled. Antonelli came again with the high, tight fastball. Aaron hit it 450 feet into the top deck of County Stadium. When the 13-3 rout of the Giants had ended, Aaron had three home runs, a double, seven RBIs, and a reputation as a guy who couldn't be intimidated.

Nor could Milwaukee, breathing hot on its first championship and weathering an early August storm that sunk the other four teams chasing the pennant. While St. Louis, Cincinnati, Brooklyn and Philadelphia were all foundering—the Phillies losing 20 of 27 games—the Braves stormed the ramparts. On August 10 they triggered a 10-game winning streak, then won seven of their next nine to take first place firmly in hand. And they had done so by overcoming several handicaps. Centerfielder Billy Bruton and shortstop Felix Mantilla collided chasing a fly ball in July, and torn knee ligaments ended Bruton's season.

There was no ceremony, but the day after Bruton had been rendered *hors de combat*, Aaron moved to center and a minor-league retread, Bob Hazle, moved into the lineup in right field. Surrounded by inartistic outfield partners, Aaron's hitting suffered and thoughts of a possible triple crown perished. Before making the switch to center, Aaron led the National League in the three most important categories: average (.340), home runs (30) and RBIs (75).

"Watching a guy like Billy Bruton play centerfield closeup gave me an inferiority complex," Aaron said. "I felt like Raggedy Andy."

Something effected Aaron's power-hitting. On July 4th, he was only two games behind the pace Babe Ruth set when he hit 60 home runs, which wasn't too bad for a guy who wanted "only to be known as a singles hitter." In any case, Aaron's bat cooled enough that the chance to challenge Ruth died. "I can't blame it on anybody but myself, but I'll tell you that playing with Wes Covington on one side of me and "Hurricane" Hazle on the other didn't give me a lot of confidence."

Hazle, however, gave the Braves as a whole a world of

confidence after arriving from Wichita following Bruton's injury. Named after a recent hurricane (right, Hazel), he carried the Braves through a stretch run with the Cards, who had taken 10 of 12 while Milwaukee was losing 8 of 11 early in September to chop the Braves' lead to 2½ games.

Hitting .330, Aaron marveled at Hazle. "He batted .403, hit seven home runs and drove in twenty-seven," Aaron said. "He was unbelievable. He made me feel like I was in a slump."

The pennant race came to crunch the third week in September and the Braves came home to County Stadium September 23 for a series against St. Louis needing only one win over the Cards to lock it up.

The tension of the race had united the Braves. It was perhaps the force that would keep them atop the National League again the following year and would hold them in the running until old age and front-office infighting destroyed the team.

"I never said Fred Haney was one of my favorite people, but I did feel something for Haney," Aaron said. "He never let us forget we were players and he was the manager. But I remembered Johnny Logan saying Haney had looked sick; that if we blew it, he probably wouldn't be back the next year."

The Braves did not blow it. Their roller-coaster dimension was gone. The opening game in the series with the Cardinals went into the 11th inning tied, 2–2, Burdette dueling the Cards' Billy Muffett, a reliever fresh from the minors.

Facing Aaron in the 11th, Muffett came with the slow curveball that was his money pitch. Aaron leveled the 32-ounce bat and brought it around in a blur. Cardinal centerfielder Wally Moon turned and raced for the base of the wall in dead center. He leaped. At precisely 11:34 p.m., C. S. T., the ball disappeared into the seats. Mil-

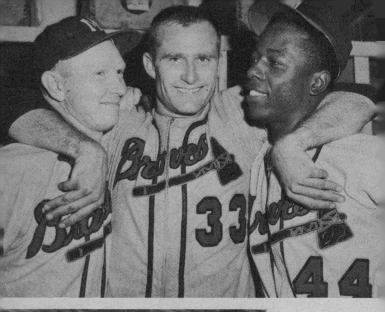

Red Schoendienst, Lew Burdette and Hank share a victory over the Brooklyn Dodgers.

Johnny Logan pours the stuff that pennants are made of after Hank's homer clinches pennant.

waukee exploded, fans pouring onto the playing surface to carry Aaron off the field triumphantly. No home run would ever be sweeter to Aaron than the one which clinched the 1957 pennant, and more than a decade later it would remain his favorite hit, although the following night he hit career No. 110, his first grand slam and the one which gave him the 1957 National League home run title. But after No. 109, in their first spontaneous show of affection for him, the fans of Milwaukee tugged him to their collective breast.

"That was my shiningest hour," he would say later. "My first thought was Bobby Thomson's homer. That had always been my idea of the most important homer. Now I got one for myself. For me to get the hit myself . . . I was excited for the first time in my whole life."

The excitement wore on for weeks. The Braves and the New York Yankees alternated wins in the first six games of the World Series, Aaron hitting almost .400 and getting a lot of ink for the first time. The world was discovering the Yankees' 1952 desire for a successor to Babe Ruth was costing them dearly five years later.

In 1952, while he was burning up the Negro American League with the Indianapolis Clowns, Aaron's initial contact with a major league club had been with the Yankees. "Some scout gave me some vague promises, but he never offered me any money. I think they really didn't want a black player."

Amidst a streak that had brought five straight pennants, the Yankees wanted a left-handed power hitter à la Ruth to shoot at the right field stands at Yankee Stadium, only 296 feet from home plate. After a cursory look, they ignored Aaron.

Five years later, they could ignore him no longer. Aaron got two of the Braves' five hits in the opening game defeat; scored their first run after tripling in the second game. He hit home runs on each of the next two days. In the fifth game, he had a key single; in the sixth a tape-measure home run. In the winning game he singled twice and drove in an important run. Now Yogi Berra understood what Aaron had told him in the first game.

"Hey, kid, you're holding the bat wrong," Berra had said. "You're supposed to have the trademark up."

"Why? I didn't come up here to read. I came up here to hit."

Aaron hit .393 in the series, getting 11 hits and 22 total bases, and he drove in seven runs and scored five more. His series performance capped a brilliant year in which he had led the league in home runs (44) and RBIs (132) while batting .322. At home his performance had been no less spectacular, as he fathered two sons in the year 1957, Henry Jr. on March 10th and Larry on December 15.

On November 14, he was in Chicago to do some promotional work for the Miller Brewing Company. Around midnight, the phone rang in his hotel room. A Chicago sportswriter wanted to send a photographer over to Aaron's hotel for a picture.

"Why?"

"Haven't you heard?" the writer asked.

"What?"

"Let me be the first to congratulate you. You've been voted the Most Valuable Player in the National League."

Aaron had edged Stan Musial in the balloting by nine votes, pretty heady stuff for the kid who had left Mobile with a cardboard suitcase and two dollars. But Henry Aaron was Henry Aaron.

"If I had told that fellow I was surprised, I'd have been a liar," he said. "I thought I had a good shot at it." Talking with the writer, he remembered the train ride from Mobile to Winston-Salem, N. C., remembered strolling

Hank and Barbara Aaron are in a Mobile Mardi Gras parade that featured King Hank, MVP.

The young slugger became the father of twin boys, prematurely born and in incubators here.

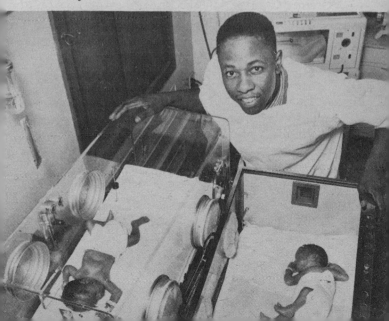

through the dining car and being surprised because "I really didn't know people sat down and ate their dinner off a table while the train was moving."

Now Henry Aaron was moving. Into the consciousness of baseball people, if not the general public.

The Braves were moving, too. On a different course.

7

The Beer Went Flat . . .

As the years fell away, with the Milwaukee club succumbing to the aging process and the front-office maneuverings that follow it as the night follows the day, Henry Aaron came to epitomize the Braves. They became, plummeting from the zenith of another pennant in 1958 to a 5th-place finish in 1962, sort of an extension of him.

He was the Milwaukee Braves. More than the persistent reliability of a Spahn refusing to erode; more than the laconic Burdette's flights of brilliance burdened by stretches of inconsistency; more than a tiring Crandall or a fading Schoendienst or a flamed-out Logan, Aaron *was* the Braves.

And as they crumbled, he stood shock still in the ruins, something of excellence to which the rapidly disillusioned Milwaukee fans could cling.

They were, these World Champions soon seized by death throes, still a hitting, slugging club as the 1950s ended and the 1960s began. Aaron was a hitter, a slugger of increasing proportions. They did not bunt; he disdained the cheapness of the bunt. They did not run; he could, but did not. As the Braves fell to the task of rebuilding, Henry Aaron swung away, the new foundation. "I've got a bat; all the pitcher's got is the ball," he said often. "I figure that gives me an edge."

Indeed. And in the years 1958 through 1962, the Braves came decidedly to lean on that edge. From the outset of the 1958 season, the Braves felt the Dodgers hot at their heels. Brooklyn had dropped clear to seventh place during the year of the Braves' greatest triumph, but now they were flying back in pursuit.

Milwaukee led the pennant chase early on, dropped to second for two weeks in June, and then from the 4th of July, it was nothing so much as two dogs and one bone.

There were indications early in the season that Milwaukee was in trouble. Injuries piled up and rarely could Haney field all of his regulars for more than one or two games at a time. Buhl developed shoulder trouble in May, was lost until September. Schoendienst broke a finger in July; his replacement, Mel Roach, was hitting over .300 when he tore up a knee the first week in August. Bruton recovered slowly from the previous season's injury and was not available until late May. Wes Covington labored on two arthritic knees.

The Braves struggled on, Aaron as steady as ever, but they were involved in the hottest National League pennant race since 1900. Until the first week in August, the last-place team was never more than 9½ games off the lead. Spahn and Burdette staggered at mid-season; rookies Joey Jay and Carlton Willey took up the slack, winning 16 between them. When Burdette finally got untracked after losing 7 of his first 13 decisions, the Braves beat back first San Francisco, and then Pittsburgh. The rawboned righthander won 14 of his last 17 starts and the

Braves breezed home by 8½ lengths to nail down a second successive pennant.

As they did, the enigma that was Henry Aaron seemed to mesmerize baseball people, who were eager to find in his unorthodox style at the plate an answer to why his home run production had dropped from 44 to 30 and his RBIs from 132 to 95.

Some experts wanted him to bunt more; others to choose his pitches more solicitously; yet others to study his art more vigorously. When Aaron said, "My daddy always told me, 'Henry, never hurry unless you have to,'" his detractors questioned his intelligence.

Aaron was unmoved by the interest he had begun to stir. "Whatever I'm doing, I don't want to know what it is. I just want to keep on doing it."

When the questions irritated him, he would retreat into drollness. "I just grab a bat and go up to the plate looking for one thing—the ball," he would say. "I've got two bats now. A long one and a short one. I use the long one when they're pitching me outside and the short one when they are pitching me inside."

His attempts at humor dissuaded no one, and everybody from Rogers Hornsby to Stan Musial was ever so sure as to what was right, or what was wrong, with Hank Aaron, hitter.

"A pitch with something on it, right across the letters and in close," was Aaron's weakness, thought Hornsby. "He still thinks there's nothing he can't hit, but there's still some pitches no hitter can afford to go for," said Musial, who once described Aaron's batting style as "arrogant."

Cincinnati's powerful first baseman Ted Kluszewski and respected Pittsburgh pitcher Bob Friend spoke for the defense. "Any pitcher in the league would gladly give him first base to keep him from getting more," Big

Klu scoffed at the suggestion that Aaron should bunt more often. "Their biggest fear is that he'll break up the game, and he won't do that with a bunt. He can't hurt you much with a bunt, but he can hurt you 8 out of 10 times when he's swinging for that long ball."

Observed Friend: "Those wrist hitters just don't have the weaknesses other hitters have. The best thing you can do is keep the ball where he'll only hit singles." The debate amused Spahn. "It's fantastic how long Henry can look at a pitch. It's like giving him an extra strike."

On the matter of Aaron's intelligence, one major-league manager laughed, "Yeah, he's dumb—like a fox. He stands there looking sleepy, and some guys get suckered."

When his failure to bunt was mentioned, Aaron merely shook his head. Years before, Jackie Robinson had advised against it. "One time I made like I was going to bunt and Robinson—he was playing third then—never moved. So I tried it again and he still didn't move. Later I asked him why. He said, 'Listen, any time you want to bunt, we'll give you first base, just so you don't get anything more.'

"He was tellin' me not to bunt, and when Jackie Robinson gives me advice like that, I listen."

During the years of the Braves' early trials, Aaron became a focal point. They lost the series to the Yankees in seven games in 1958, and it signaled the organization's downfall, at least to Aaron. "I couldn't recognize it as it was happening," he said later, "but after the 1957 series when we beat New York, everything else for the Braves in Milwaukee went downhill."

And so it did. Aaron rolled on as the 1950s faded and the '60s began. In 1959, he led the league for the second time by hitting .355, which included 39 home runs and 123 RBIs. Impressive statistics, but not enough to prevent the beginnings of the Milwaukee tailspin.

The Dodgers, moved to Los Angeles, replaced the

Warren Spahn and Hank show their respective Cy Young and MVP plaques.

A Braves-Yankees exhibition game brought together MVPs Mickey Mantle and Hank Aaron in 1958.

Braves as the team of the future. Getting away to one of the fast starts which had become their trademark, the Braves led the league by 4½ games in mid-May, but dropped 15 of 29 in July. Still, when the noose of a second straight tight race tightened, Milwaukee refused to choke.

The Braves won 15 of 20 and when Los Angeles stumbled in the last week, Milwaukee forced a playoff on the strength of Bob Buhl's masterful 5-2 win over Philadelphia in the final game of the season.

But the stretch run had burned out the Braves and they lost the playoff in two games, bowing 3-2 and 6-5 to the Dodgers. The slide which would not end for 10 years had begun. Over the course of the next few seasons, the Braves seemed to sink into the lower depths of the National League, leaving only Aaron and the ageless Spahn visible to the baseball public.

Clearly reorganization was necessary and no one felt it keener than Fred Haney, who resigned after the playoff defeat. A new man had come to the fore in the Milwaukee front office. Birdie Tebbets, who had resigned or been fired as the Cincinnati field manager the year before, was hired as the Braves' executive vice president. John Quinn, an old baseball hand, quickly smelled the winds of change and resigned, going to Philadelphia as general manager. The shakeup was completed when youthful John McHale, who held the general manager's job in Detroit, replaced Quinn and the venerable Charlie Dressen was hired as manager. To top things off, Lou Perini sold the club to a Chicago-based group headed by young Bill Bartholomay.

One of the game's great characters, Dressen wore rough on the Braves, most of whom had come to like and respect the tough Haney. Regarding himself as the key component to his team, Dressen immediately made it clear that he might just be the difference between a pennant and disaster in 1960. Perhaps he was. "Keep 'em close and I'll think of something," Dressen had once told a contending team in a difficult game. It was his managerial philosophy, but the Braves never bought it.

"He'd wear you out with his brilliance," Aaron observed drily as the 1960 Braves were beginning to come apart. A .500 team much of the year, they made a charge in late June, winning 19 of 26 games to move into second place behind front-running Pittsburgh. But in July they died ingloriously, a seven-game losing streak taking them out of the chase for good.

A year later Milwaukee was a run of the mill club. Spahn won his 300th in 1961, but after winning 10 consecutive games during a mid-August home stand, the Braves faltered and dropped a notch to finish fourth, 10 games behind the pennant-winning Cincinnati Reds.

Tebbetts had ineffectually sought to stem the tide personally that season, firing Dressen early in September and moving on to the bench. He decided to manage again in 1962, but the degeneration was complete by then and Milwaukee fell all the way to fifth place, trailing the champion San Francisco Giants by a full 15½ games. En route, Tebbetts managed to earn the enmity of most of the older Braves, including Aaron, whom he fined for being late for a plane to New York.

"I still get hot flashes when I think about it," Aaron said later. He had stopped to pick up rookie infielder Amado Samuel en route to the airport and they had a flat tire while riding along a freeway.

"What the hell, haven't you heard of the telephone?" Tebbetts smoldered when Aaron and Samuel arrived at the airport. Aaron explained. "Birdie, there aren't many phones on the freeway." That, Tebbetts retaliated, didn't make any difference. "It'll cost you," he told Aaron. "You'll learn that nobody's a star on this team."

Aaron, who had never received anything even resembling special privileges from the Braves, didn't forget the incident. "Birdie's not the kind of a guy I'd die for," he deadpanned.

During the years 1958-1962 and the decaying of the Braves, Aaron rolled along like Old Man River, his statistics almost an unwavering line of excellence. In 1959, he led the league in hitting again with a .355 average, and with the exception of 1960 when he batted .292, his lowest average was .326. During that five-year span, he hit 188 home runs and averaged 118 RBIs a season, leading the league in 1960. He started every All-Star Game during those years and acquired three Gold Gloves for fielding excellence.

But he, too, remained somewhat puzzled as to what had occurred to the Braves. "We had all grown complacent," he said. "We could never perform at our best unless we had our backs to the wall. I couldn't recognize it as it was happening. You can't blame that on my youth. There were a lot of people older, wiser, and more experienced than Henry Aaron who were living right in the middle of it and couldn't recognize it, either. But after the 1957 World Series, everything seemed to go downhill, everything seemed in decline. We were losing a little of what we had but we didn't know it until it was too late to do anything about it. I don't blame it on any particular group—the managers or the front office or the players. We all had our part in it. It was a team disaster."

But not necessarily a personal disaster to Hank Aaron. Hank. Not Henry. Henry had gone by then, victim of the fertile mind of Donald Davidson, the Braves' traveling secretary who dubbed Aaron "Hank" in an attempt to give him more of what baseball likes to call "color."

Hank Aaron stayed upright as the Braves fell on their collective faces. In 1959, it was Aaron whose bat carried Milwaukee in pursuit of Los Angeles. As late as early July, the big question in baseball was: Will Aaron be-

100

come the first man in 18 years to bat .400? No longer was he regarded as the yawning young man with the natural bat.

"Yeah, Hank's just asleep up there," Brave catcher Del Crandall mocked an old theory. "He knows nothing. Sure. All he knows is about every pitch that any pitcher ever got him out on. The next time the same pitcher tries the same pitch, he hits it out of sight. Sure he was fooled some when he first came up. But nobody's fooling Hank much any more."

Certainly in the spring of 1959, the National League pitchers weren't. Aaron hit .487 in his first 27 games, getting at least two hits in 20 of them. On May 16th, it would have been possible for him to have gone hitless in his next 56 times at bat and still have been hitting .333. He had given his unconscionable bat even more freedom and the pitchers had not taken note.

"I'm not waiting for certain pitches any more," he explained. "I'm going out after the ball. Last year I was waiting for particular pitches and getting behind, then they'd give me a curve in the dirt and I'd be in trouble. I can't wait for a certain pitch. Most of the balls I hit real good are outside of the strike zone. Why, I've never hit a 3-0 pitch in my life. I know right where the pitcher's going to throw it and I still pop it up."

The question of Aaron's ability to maintain a plus .400 average throughout the season drew heavy debate. Rogers Hornsby, whose .424 average in 1924 remained a major-league high and who was one of only eight players to ever reach that exalted plateau, was called upon as an expert witness.

"With the start he has, he could hit .400," Hornsby said. "He has become a better hitter than ever because he's gotten more confidence. Call it poise, or experience, but he pays more attention to the strike zone. He hits with power to all fields, and that's the test of a hitter."

Braves' manager Fred Haney, of course, was called to testify. "Maybe he'll only hit .360. Maybe he will hit .400. I don't know. He's capable of anything."

Tebbetts, at the time about to give up his managerial duties in Cincinnati, airily said, "He could win the batting title for the next five or six years if he gets to be a well-rounded hitter instead of just being a natural hitter."

In June, still above the magic mark, Aaron collected basehit No. 1000, at age 25, younger than seven of the eight immortals who stayed around to record their 3000th. If he could avoid prolonged slumps, he said then, he could perhaps top the .406 Ted Wiliams had registered in 1941.

"I can do it," he said. "All I need to do is stay as hot as I am. And a little luck would help. I'm certainly off to the best start of my career. If I'm ever going to do, this has to be the year."

It wasn't. The long, hot summer caught up to Aaron and in August his bat cooled considerably. Still, he finished at .355, the highest average in the majors that year.

As the Braves plummeted in 1960, Aaron's bat remained cooler than usual, although he hit 40 home runs and led the league with 126 RBIs. But his average fell to .292, a shade low for a $55,000 a year hitter. He was being lured into hitting outside breaking balls by right-handed pitchers, who held him to a .272 mark while he was swatting lefthanders at a .346 clip.

"When I was with the Dodgers, I used to shudder when he came to bat," said Braves' manager Charlie Dressen, "but this year they're throwing lollypops and getting him out."

Dressen, himself, may have contributed to Aaron's poor year. Early in training camp, with the aging Schoendienst and untried Chuck Cottier the only second basemen on the roster, Dressen said he might use Aaron at the position. Aaron didn't think much of the idea.

"If he tells me to, I'll go back to second base," Aaron said, "and I'll do the best I can. All I ask is that I play there in the spring. I don't want to go there at mid-season and be made a fool of at the position."

Dressen wouldn't make a decision during training camp, keeping Aaron in suspense until June before completely junking the idea.

Aaron's batting eye returned during the off-season when he won $15,000 in a televised home run hitting contest, although he had to use $1,000 of the prize money to pay a fine. He failed to play for a team of major-leaguers barnstorming through the South with the sanction of the commissioner's office. Aaron's failure to heed the contract cost him $1,000 after his appeal to Commissioner Ford Frick had been rejected. "It was hard to take," Aaron bristled later. "I had been having back troubles and I sent the league office a medical report showing why I wasn't playing."

After paying the fine, Aaron spent the rest of the winter campaigning in behalf of presidential candidate John F. Kennedy and getting ready for the 1961 season, during which he would extract a measure of revenge from National League pitchers.

Before he could busy himself with that task, however, he and Birdie Tebbetts had another clash. This time over housing for black players at the Bradenton training site.

Years of living in an overcrowded boarding house in the black section of Bradenton finally palled on Aaron in the spring of 1961 and he took exception to Tebbetts' published remarks that the black Braves were happy with their accommodations "in a carefully selected private home."

"Carefully selected from what?" Aaron exploded to Milwaukee baseball writer Bob Wolf. "There's not but one place down here for us to stay in. It's the only one where we can eat, and that's kind of important. But sometimes this place is so crowded they have two guys sleeping in the hall. We're playing together, why not live together?"

Admonished, the Braves agreed to shift to a hotel where blacks were accepted and Hank Aaron proceeded to do his usual number on the National League, rebuilding his average to .327, pumping out 34 home runs and driving in 120.

The following year the disintegration of the Braves seemed to become complete. The Milwaukee fans—their initial love affair with the Braves going on the rocks as early as 1959 when only 18,297 people showed at County Stadium for the first playoff game with the Dodgers— began to stay away in droves.

Desperate, Milwaukee management decided the club needed a new look and instituted a series of trades, letting go such old-time favorites as Johnny Logan, Red Schoendienst, Joey Jay, Juan Pizarro and Billy Bruton.

The loss of his best friend, Bruton, disheartened Aaron. "Faces seemed to change every week. Players came and went like livestock. As the old favorites began disappearing, the replacements never really caught on with the fans. And if there was anything those Milwaukee fans liked to be reminded of, it was those good years when we had been winning pennants."

To worsen matters, the Braves refused to allow their fans to drag to the ballpark the ice chests filled with beer that had become an institution of Milwaukee baseball. The town that made beer famous reacted as if the regulation banning its brew was treasonable and attendance sagged more than ever, dropping to a low point of 766,-000 in 1962.

The fans that did support the Braves had to be content with Hank Aaron and a weak supporting cast. In 1962,

Roberto Clemente, Willie Mays and Aaron celebrate National League All-Star victory in San Francisco in 1961.

Hank is joined by brother Tommy, spring training, 1962.

Aaron hit .328, drove in 123 runs and ripped a career high 45 home runs. Still, the Braves faltered, playing just 10 games over .500 and finishing 15½ games off the pace.

Once more reorganization was deemed necessary. Tebbetts returned to the desk in favor of the zany Bobby Bragan. Another era had begun. The Braves would not survive it in Milwaukee, bringing grief to Henry Aaron, whose conscience would soon tug at him as it never had before.

8

The Pride of a Loner

As a chilling late autumn wind hurtles across the South Dakota flatlands, a rangy 17-year-old, his eyes vacant and troubled, and a slim, broad-shouldered man toss a baseball back and forth behind a state mental hospital. The boy approaches the man and suddenly drives the baseball at the man's face. The boy's arm is caught in a gentle vise inches from the man's eyes. "That's just fine," the man smiles. "You threw the ball fine. Tomorrow we'll try it again."

The man's name is Henry Aaron.

A rookie baseball writer walks into the Braves' clubhouse. He is a 31-year-old man, the father of two children, he reminds himself, both embarrassed and annoyed at being nervous. He approaches the superstar, who this season will make what it will take the rookie baseball writer six years to earn. The superstar walks the length of the clubhouse to get the writer a chair.

The superstar's name is Henry Aaron.

Ricardo Adolfo Jacobo Carty is a rookie. He knows

few words of English. He is playing poorly and because of it is so nervous he cannot sleep or eat. A veteran observes Carty and asks the manager if they can room together. The next day the nervous rookie says of the veteran, "Already he is showing me how to talk better, how to act, what to wear. He is my best *compadre*. He is even showing me about hitting."

The veteran's name is Henry Aaron.

In a hotel lobby, a large drunk is annoying two women and blocking the exit. His language is crude. Other men pretend not to notice. A newcomer walks into the lobby and heads for the door. "Please get out of my way," he says to the drunk. He is cursed. He grabs a handful of shirt and slams the drunk against a stone pillar. "Now move."

The newcomer's name is Henry Aaron.

A reporter who has known the outfielder for years and is his friend, says candidly, "I don't think anyone really knows him. But maybe everyone does. Maybe he is exactly what he appears to be."

The outfielder's name is Henry Aaron.

And what does Henry Aaron appear to be? A self-contained man. Infinitely private, yet open and friendly. Reserved, yet warm. Certainly not a true wit, but just as surely a man not devoid of humor. A man who does his own bidding, his own grieving. Quietly religious, publicly thrifty. Black, but not with a capital B. Proud. Extraordinarily proud, for a man without a driving pride could have never reached such heights. Sociable, but never in public.

But, mostly, unknown. A riddle. The Henry Aaron Doll. Wind it up and it hits a home run and then, poof, disappears. The only legend that is also a nonentity.

Or, perhaps, Aaron is merely what most of us are, something of a paradox. From the day he realized he had been bilked by the financial agreement between the Indianapolis Clowns and the Milwaukee Braves, Aaron pursued the dollar mightily. In 1963, he was determinedly negotiating a $60,000 a year contract from the Braves. But it was said of Aaron that he still had the first dollar he'd ever made, and he drove a Ford, and his home in suburban Mequon was comfortable but hardly ostentatious, a place Ruth would've regarded as low-income housing.

"I heard some talk that I'm cheap when it comes to tipping," Aaron said. "Sure, Aaron the rich star should tip a buck everywhere. But I don't. I've got some businesses and real estate property, and that's where my spare money goes. All of my kids are going to college."

Fine. Thrift is a virtue. But Aaron never sought the endorsements which could've considerably increased his earnings. "Those big talent agents get you and divide your mind," he said. "You get to thinking about things other than hitting. And soon you don't know your own kids from your neighbors'. My spare time is theirs. I don't golf or go to nightclubs much."

Because he was such a private man, few people got to know Aaron intimately and in time he became taken for granted, as music and spring and the stars are taken for granted. He was untouched by any investigation of his personality and no one ever seemed to know or care that he could fall in love in the summer, or that he converted to Catholicism because it was a more convenient way for a ballplayer to worship, or that he had arthritis in his neck, or was a connoisseur of Chinese food.

He was merely Henry Aaron and there was about him something unapproachable, a look, a way of carrying himself, a glint in his eyes, something.

"I can't tell you if he's married or what town he lives in," said the Dodgers' Tommy Davis. "All I know about him is that he waits on the pitched ball better than anyone I ever saw, moves any kind of a pitch in more directions than any of us, and is the best man in the world with a bat. The players just call him 'The Workman,' or 'Wrists,' or 'The Most,' or '44.' "

Aaron's ability to lead a private life all but awed Eddie Mathews. "They seem to realize he's a tremendous individualist who prefers and needs to be left alone," Mathews said. "And, by golly, the fans just part like the sea to let him pass. A terrific compliment. There's been times they've been tearing off my shirt and Spahn's for autographs when we've envied this thing Henry's got with the public." Whatever the thing was, it is perhaps the reason that the fans have, shockingly, considering his contributions, never elected him the "Most Popular Brave."

In no way an unfriendly man, Aaron still did not parade his problems or his philosophy. In 1957, he went through a trying season, but it was years before even his good friends knew how trying. "He never said much about it, but he went through hell that year," said Spahn. "He lost a baby and we still don't know much of the details." The details were that Barbara Aaron gave birth prematurely to twins, Larry and Gary, and Gary died the day after birth.

Yet the paradox persists. Men who will not share of themselves do not usually get on well with the young. But Aaron—privately, of course—does. Each winter he would slip off to Dolan, South Dakota, to hunt pheasants with a former minor league pitcher named Lefty Miller. While there, he did enough work at the state mental hospital that in the winter of 1963, state senator Pat Keel said from the floor of the South Dakota legislature, "Gentlemen, I don't know of any public figure who takes a stronger interest in the handicapped young than this young man from baseball."

For years, Braves' radio announcer Ernie Johnson had

110

been dropping by the Milwaukee Children's Hospital. One day in 1963, he called Aaron to ask if he'd visit a boy dying of cancer. When they walked into the young patient's ward, the boy yelled "there's Hank, I know him." Johnson thought the boy had recognized Aaron from television. "No," he was told, "Hank's been coming here to see the children for years."

In an attempt to total the sum of Aaron's personality, one reporter wrote, "He is a clean movie with a good ending." If so, the movie would have to be at least partly a comedy, because Aaron is not a dour man. Asked his most important function with the Braves, Aaron instantly grinned, "Chasing pitcher's mistakes." Occasionally he brings his wit to the field, as he did the night he told a catcher who was berating an umpire, "Kindly do not agitate the arbiter. He cannot be as pluperfect as you are."

Braves' general manager John McHale attests to Aaron's wit. Informed that Aaron had hurt his back, McHale quickly called the Aaron home with visions of a bent and crippled superstar only to be told, "It's not so bad. It doesn't hurt when I swing, only when I kneel in church."

Although Aaron has never indicated it publicly, there is a suspicion that his detachment has been fostered by his religious beliefs and aids him as a performer. Estella and Herbert Aaron are staunch Baptists, but Henry became the family's only Catholic because baseball prevented him from carrying out the responsibilities of his faith.

"Hank's a very unusual human being," said the Rev. Michael Sablica, a philosophy professor whose influence was at least partly responsible for Aaron's conversion. "He has a naturally good mind and you can't help sensing his consciousness has evolved to a high level. His mental and emotional preparation for a game is remarkable."

If a single personality trait could be said to drive Aaron, most of the people who know him well agree it is pride. "That's the single best word to describe Henry Aaron . . . proud," said a friend. "I think that pride is what makes him a loner. And he is. I don't know of a single player that you could honestly say Henry's been close to."

Aaron agrees he is proud. "Pride helps everybody. I take pride in what I'm doing every day I go out there. I know there will be bad days and bad games, but I want to be consistent. That's pride. And you have to have it in baseball. You're out there everyday with the best there is."

If Aaron is possessed of single personality trait that does not seem to fall in place with others he owns, it is his tendency to carry a grudge. Aaron does not forget. His salary negotiations have lacked some of the amiability with which other superstars have reached six-figure contracts. He remembers people "taking advantage of a poor colored boy." And years after the incident occurred, he smoldered at remembering being disciplined by Fred Haney. "I've never forgotten it. I've always thought about it."

But perhaps the best judgment of a man and his character and his personality is to be found in the observations of others. To some he is a robot. Said a teammate once, "He's human. He's not a machine . . . although come to think of it there seems to be some doubt about that."

Although they are polarized personalities, Eddie Mathews and Leo Durocher see in Aaron a powerful constancy of play and life-style. "A super guy," said Mathews. "He hasn't changed an inch."

"He has class," observed Durocher, who spends compliments as though they are negotiable. "His class is based

112

on quiet competence, lacking in emotional outbursts so that only the wiser heads accept him for what he is, one of the greatest. And I mean the all-time greatest."

All play and no work make for a dull boy, and Aaron knows how to play. But he does it as he does all manner of things, quietly and privately. "A lot of players have favorite bars," said Eddie Mathews. "They meet there, then take off in different directions. The next day in the clubhouse, guys would be telling about the women they'd had or how much they drank. I used to ask Henry where he went and he just smiled and said, 'out.'"

When visiting baseball teams hit New York, most of the black players head for The Red Rooster at 137th Street and Seventh Avenue in Harlem. Willie Mays is the crowd favorite at the Red Rooster. No one bothers about Aaron. "If he's here, he never has a drink or a beer in front of him," sighs Mike Simms, the bartender. But Mays and Aaron are polarized personalities. Mays drives a pink Chrysler with "Say, Hey" license plates; Aaron gets around in a modest blue sedan.

"He knows how to have fun and when he was single he had his share of women," said a writer who knows Aaron well. "But above everything else, Henry does not want to be embarrassed on or off the field."

While the Braves were being so embarrassed that in time they would have to flee Milwaukee red-faced, Henry Aaron did nothing to humiliate himself. The Braves continued to languish in mediocrity during the 1963, 1964 and 1965 campaigns, but that had precious little to do with Aaron. As they lay submerged in the second division in 1963 under new manager Bobby Bragan, Aaron was making another run at the triple crown.

Bragan could do nothing to stem the Braves' rush from the top of the National League standings to near the bottom. Subdued in Milwaukee—while managing Pittsburgh he frequently stretched out in the third-base coaching box, offered soft drinks to the umpires, and on one memorable occasion had a bucket of water delivered to the mound to a pitcher he suspected of throwing a spitball—Bragan became an Aaron favorite.

"It was sort of a mutual kind of respect," Aaron said after the Braves had lost 11 of 13 games in early May to drop out of the pack of teams that were chasing the Dodgers to the 1963 pennant. "I got along well with him, although some of the other guys didn't."

It was Bragan who first suspected Aaron could become the sort of home run hitter to challenge even Ruth. "Like Jimmy Foxx and some of those power hitters of the past, he hits a ball that takes off. You know how you can hit a golf ball that will stay about 10 feet off the ground for 50 yards or so and then climb and go for distance? Well, that's the way Aaron hits a baseball."

He certainly hit it that way in 1963, although it didn't help the Braves who, after winning 22 of 28 games in August to leap into third place, lost their last eight and finished sixth. While the enduring Spahn was hanging up an incredible 23-7 record at age 42, Aaron narrowly missed the triple crown. He led the league with 130 RBIs and tied San Francisco's Willie McCovey with 44 home runs, one of which was No. 300, but was seven points shy of Tommy Davis' league-leading .319 average. Dodger manager Walt Alston was unmoved.

"Forget statistics," he said. "It's the conviction of most managers that Aaron wins more ball games than any guy since maybe Hornsby in his prime. One night in August we concentrated on stopping *him*. I mean we gave it the works. We gave him nothing but bad pitches. We jammed him and dusted him. We worked every trick to pick him off base. When he slid, we got rough with him.

"So he winds up with two singles and a home run, stole a base, robbed us of a triple with a hell of a catch, accounted for four runs and beat us from here to Toledo. More times than anyone else, he's made me wish I wasn't a manager."

In 1963, Aaron was one of the few reasons Bragan was glad he was a manager. Given the green light to run, Aaron stole 31 bases, thus becoming one of only five players in history to hit more than 30 home runs and steal more than 30 times in a single season. And he shouldered the further decay of the Braves without losing his sense of humor. Routed from his hotel room by a fire, Aaron was asked by a policeman if he was all right. "Yeah, but if I go 0-for-4, I'll say I wasn't."

The following season, Aaron, and the Braves, could have used an excuse. The Braves played poorly, needing to take 20 of their last 26 games to finish a respectable 14 games over the .500 mark and finish fifth, five games behind pennant-winning St. Louis. Capitalizing on a total collapse by Philadelphia—with the championship all but locked away, the Phils dropped 10 straight—St. Louis won the pennant on the final day of the season. Aaron was not much better than the Braves as a unit, although he became an all-star for the 13th consecutive time on the strength of a batting average that closed at .328. But he drove in only 95 runs, his lowest total in eight seasons, and hit only 24 home runs, the least he had authored since his rookie season a decade before.

Neither Bragan or the clown princes of baseball, the New York Mets, worried over Aaron's sub-par season. During the winter of 1964, the Mets offered Milwaukee a half-million dollars for Aaron and were turned down, although it is a good thing Aaron wasn't personally consulted. Strong rumors that the club was heading South to Atlanta in 1965 bothered him. "I just won't step out on the field in Atlanta," he said, recalling the nights of abuse in Montgomery and other Southern cities. "I certainly

Joe DiMaggio receives Sultan of Swat crown and Hank is honored as the Slugger of 1963 by Maryland Professional Baseball Players Association.

don't like the idea of playing there and I have no intentions of taking my family to Atlanta."

Bragan was nauseated by the Mets' offer for Aaron. A manager who often used reporters and was not above framing quotes with big, bold headlines in mind, Bragan took every opportunity to lavish praise on Aaron during the winter of 1964.

"I wouldn't dream of trading Aaron for Willie Mays," he said, only days after attaching "at least a million-dollar" price tag on his ace. "When Aaron stole 31 bases, he became the complete ballplayer. Until last year, Mays had the edge over Henry on defense and base-running. Now Henry is probably the better runner."

Considering that Mays was making almost double Aaron's $60,000 salary, Bragan's comments were widely challenged. The Braves' manager stood firm. "Everybody agrees Henry is the better hitter. Pitchers would rather face Mays. Willie generates more excitement than Henry. Aaron is like Joe DiMaggio in that respect. He does everything matter-of-factly, with a minimum of exertion. Things come easy to him."

Things came easy to neither Aaron nor Bragan nor the Braves in 1965, although Aaron easily suffered the least. While his 32 home runs were high on a club that set a major-league record by having six players hit 20 or more, and while his average was a solid .328, Aaron drove in only 89 runs, his low since 1954.

Meanwhile, the Braves had fallen into their old habit of inconsistency. Surging twice—winning 10 straight in July and 11 of 13 in August—they were only two games behind first-place Los Angeles entering September. But during the stretch run, playing in front of fans cleverly disguised as empty seats due to the impending move to Atlanta, the Braves collapsed and closed 11 games off the lead.

A fan boycott was threatened in May, when a night

game drew only 914 paid customers, and it was informally in effect all year. Milwaukee, which had loved the Braves like few cities ever love a baseball team, turned its back on them in 1965. In the process of drawing only 555,584 fans by late May, the club decided, threatened lawsuit or not, it would move.

Formal confirmation of the rumor touched off a blaze that almost ignited baseball. Milwaukee politicians, sensing an opportunity to win large doses of their constituents' affection, roared into battle. A lawsuit was prepared. The Braves countered by starting a fund and donating a nickel for every paid admission to finance a campaign to lure another club to Milwaukee. Milwaukee would have none of it and began litigation which enriched dozens of attorneys, captured the mind of the American public for months, and ultimately failed, although the American League moved into town a few years later.

The entire team was unsettled during 1965, as its record indicates, and there were few compensations for Aaron. He tied a record by hitting 24 home runs through June, but a troublesome ankle injury slowed that pace drastically the final three months of the season.

Also, 1965 had a startling effect on baseball history. It was the year Aaron had a home run erased from the book. In a game in St. Louis late in the 1965 season, Aaron finally got retribution against the pitcher he called "the toughest I ever faced." He ripped a Curt Simmons' curveball onto the right-field roof, only to be ruled out when Cardinal catcher Bob Uecker, later a teammate, protested Aaron had stepped out of the batter's box while swinging. Umpire Chris Pelekoudas upheld Uecker and Aaron's home run was not allowed.

"If I ever get to within one of Babe Ruth's record, I think I'll pay a little call on Mr. Uecker," Aaron laughed later, unappreciative of the incident's irony.

118

Ed Mathews and Aaron walk tunnel for the last time at Milwaukee's County Stadium as Braves carpet-bagged to Atlanta.

Shortly after the 1965 season ended, a Milwaukee civic organization had a night for Aaron, although the Braves' front office ignored it. The club had already moved its offices to Atlanta.

But there was a problem. Henry Aaron wasn't sure he was going to go with it.

9

Black Enough

Nigger. NIGGER. *Nigger!*

Sooner or later they all hear it and little black legs pump madly for home. Some cry, wounded by the oppression they sense in a word. "Mama, what's a nigger?"

No black parent ever escapes that question. Ever. What's a nigger?

In Henry Aaron's youth, it was separate water fountains and 70-year-old men being called "boy" and the inevitability of accepting the knowledge you were different, less.

But times change. A fierce, proud man named Jackie Robinson takes baseball by the scruff of the neck, snatches it close to a grim black face, and his talent and his courage and his indomitability scream, "Call me Mister."

Times change. Martin Luther King leads thousands down Highway 80 out of Selma, Alabama and the Civil Rights Movement grinds Jim Crow under its collective feet. Times change. James Baldwin writes and black kids discover Crispus Attucks and Ralph Bunche helps hold the world together a day or two longer. Times change.

And so, like the rest of us, Henry Aaron changes. But he remembers the primary lesson of his childhood. "When I was a kid I realized that if your skin is black, you're not going to be on equal terms. You have to fight a little harder when you've been told you are second best. The Negro man has been the lowest creature on earth. Even a dog gets better treatment."

The words are bitter. And why not? But there are the Jackie Robinsons and Martin Luther Kings, and their words and deeds fired an idea called Black Awareness. And times changed.

For Aaron, the inspiration was, of course, Robinson. "I think Satchel Paige said the thing that sums it all up. Could anybody else have taken the pressure? I know I couldn't. He was the model to pave the way for all blacks to get into sports. His courage and intelligence showed what a black man could be made of."

But surely, a reporter wondered of Aaron, as a boy he must've had other heroes.

"How the hell was I supposed to have a hero?" Aaron retorted. "There were no blacks in baseball. Have you ever seen a picture of Babe Ruth surrounded by black kids?" Who, then, inspired him? "Jackie Robinson and Henry Aaron."

But Jackie Robinson was not a local hero in Atlanta, where ironically the minor-league baseball team had for years been known as the "Crackers." Certainly, in 1966 it was an impressive city. Hub of the New South. Its conscience a Pulitzer Prize-winning newspaperman named Ralph McGill who refused to let the city sink into the morass of a race war that plagued the remainder of the region in the 1950s and early 1960s. Atlanta, announced Mayor Ivan Allen, was "too busy to hate." And it was true that Atlanta throbbed with industry and hummed with the sort of civic vitality that spent more than three years and millions of dollars to acquire a major-league baseball team. A nice place, Atlanta. For white people.

But Atlanta was the Deep South. To Aaron, a large, shiny Mobile. A place where black kids learned the meaning of the word nigger very early in life. He had spent 12 years in Milwaukee, where at least there was a veneer of racial equality. Should he now give up the sort of freedom that must course strongly through a black man who has escaped southern ghetto poverty? How would his wife, his children be treated in the land of Jim Crow?

And by 1966, times indeed had changed, and Henry Aaron was no longer reticent concerning injustice. Earlier in his career, he had insisted on being a baseball player, and little more. He felt no call, as he put it, "to crusade."

"I've been told I should be more of a leader, more outspoken," he said then. "I have a deaf ear to all that kind of talk. I'm a very good listener. The way I see it, my responsibility lies on the field. It doesn't go to speaking out in the newspapers. I consider myself a baseball player first, a black man second—and I'm proud of both."

There were many young blacks, in and out of baseball, who no longer could tolerate that type of personal belief after Dr. King began to march, and Aaron was criticized for not stepping to the forefront of the struggle. "He believes you accomplish more by deeds than by words," Aaron's brother-in-law, Bill Lucas, explained. "Some people are militant and some are not. Henry is conservative by nature."

But times change. And Aaron changed with them. It was a time for words, and he remembered the slurs of the Sally League and too many meals eaten on buses and being hidden away down dark corridors in too many hotels, and finally he spoke them.

"Many times we black athletes haven't spoken out," he

admitted. "I've been guilty myself. But I've learned that when you don't say anything, people think you're satisfied. I'm not talking about being violent or militant. I'm talking about standing up for what's right."

However, what's right in Milwaukee, he knew, might not necessarily be right in Atlanta. In Milwaukee, he had had no problems. The Aarons lived in a four-bedroom, $50,000 home in Mequon, a Milwaukee exurb. It was a white neighborhood and the prevailing conditions were such that one writer was prompted to observe weeks after Aaron purchased the home that "there were no stonings or cross-burnings." In time, white kids laid in wait for Aaron to return from the ballpark. "How should I hold my bat, Henry? How do you catch the high ones, Henry?" One neighbor sighed, "I don't know how he stands all the questions. He has more patience than any man I ever saw." Aaron was realistic about living in Mequon. "My neighbors are real nice, warm, friendly folks. But I don't think the average colored person could live here. They accept me because I am a baseball player, but I just want to get along with them because I'm a human being. All I want is what most people want, a decent place for my wife and kids. It doesn't make no difference if people don't want to talk to me."

But now it was not that simple. The Braves had moved to Atlanta, and Aaron was particularly suspicious of southern whites. In Bradenton, Florida, a few years before, a Buick driven by a white man had purposely driven his smaller car into a ditch, and Aaron and Felix Mantilla barely escaped with their lives. "I told some guys on the club and they said, 'Don't mention it.' The NAACP will get hold of it, and there you go....' I said, 'I almost lost my life and you want me to keep it a secret?' I mentioned it to newspapermen, but they didn't print a line about it. That's the kind of things that happens in the south to Negro ballplayers."

Aaron's awareness of racial prejudice had been well honed by 1966, and if he wasn't militant, he was outspoken, decrying the injustices he had suffered silently in the past.

"All we want is equal rights. I've read some of Baldwin's books. He says we've waited long enough. My parents are waiting right now in Alabama. The whites told my parents, 'Wait and things'll get better.' They told me, 'Wait and things'll get better.' Well, we're not going to wait any more.' "

His feelings released, Aaron vented them freely. Baseball had almost pulled its arms from the sockets patting itself on the back because it had permitted Jackie Robinson to play. But Aaron remembered that baseball had allowed blacks to be treated shoddily. In cities like St. Louis, he noticed the black Brave players never received rooms facing the outside of the hotel or the swimming pool. "We're always in a blind spot, looking at some old building or a blank wall so nobody can see us through a window. We never can look at people walking on the street, or kids playing in the pool." In St. Louis, blacks were not allowed in the dining room; in Cincinnati, no restaurants in the downtown area would serve blacks; in other hotels on the road, a screen was placed around the black players."

On the field, Aaron was thrown at unmercifully. "It goes through my head that it's because I'm a Negro. What makes me think so is that Eddie Mathews is just as much a hitter as I am, and I've batted right behind him for years and I've never seen him knocked down."

Baseball's pride in its dealings with blacks is, of course, hypocrisy at the terminal stage. There is no black manager; only token blacks in the front offices. Aaron lashed out accordingly. "Baseball is no different than stagnant water. The Negro has progressed no further than the field. Until we crack that area, there is no real hope for black kids coming into sports. We're giants on the field for twenty years; then they're finished with us. I feel that when I retire, some major-league executive should say, 'Henry I want to give you a job.' Not as a super-scout. I want a job in the front office. I ride in the front seat of the bus for years and then they say, 'Go to the back, you can't do anything else for us?'

"I don't owe baseball anything because I have played this game just as hard as anyone who has ever played it. Sure, I came out of Alabama with nothing; but a lot of front office people came out of Alabama and Mississippi with nothing. But they hung on to baseball, and I don't think they know any more about the game than I do."

Aaron's harshest criticism was reserved for baseball's failure to hire a black manager. "There's a club and the owners seem to have gotten together and decided that certain men—certain *white* men—should be hired and re-hired no matter what kind of failures they've been. Take guys like Gene Mauch or Harry Walker. They've both had real good teams at one time or another, but have never had a winner. Yet, as soon as they're fired by one owner, they're hired by another. A second chance is one thing, but when you've been lousy time and time again with first-rate material, it seems ridiculous. Especially with guys like Ernie [Banks] and Willie [Mays] available in the wings."

And how about Henry Aaron? "I think I know enough about the game and how to get along with a whole team to produce a winner. And I'd say the same about Ernie or Willie. Unfortunately, no owner has had the guts to hire a black manager. In fact, I wouldn't even call it guts. It's more common sense. It's already been proved in other sports like basketball that a black man can both produce a winner and bring in sellout crowds. It's just a question of one owner showing enough courage or decency to break the ice. I can't understand why it hasn't happened already."

But times change, because quiet men like Henry Aaron speak out. Still, somehow tragically, they do not become heroes to their people. Aaron has ripped at injustice often; Willie Mays has totally ignored it. Yet . . . "I don't think all the brothers are plugged into Hank Aaron because he's not electrifying," said a black New York journalist, Frank McRae. "He doesn't reflect the image of the 'soul man' like Willie Mays, who does everything with a lot of flair. Hank Aaron, in the minds of a lot of blacks, is not black enough."

He is black enough for the young baseball players who have followed his lead in speaking out on racial matters within the game. He is black enough for Reggie Jackson to telephone Aaron one day to say, "Thanks, we younger black players realize what you older guys have done for us."

"Hank is genuinely proud of being a black man," said a friend. "And he feels he's contributed to the cause."

In February of 1966, it was the Braves' turn to contribute. Aaron went to Atlanta to negotiate his contract and told owner Bill Bartholomay he would play there. In the spirit of the day, Bartholomay signed Aaron to a $70,000-a-year contract, second only to the 75 grand the club had given pitcher Warren Spahn in 1964.

"They did all right by me . . . and the Internal Revenue people. I got more than $600 a month they gave me for playing in Jacksonville in 1953," Aaron said, no longer the "poor colored boy" ignorant of financial matters.

For Aaron, the $70,000 contract represented considerable fiscal freedom. He had always been a rather frugal man, perhaps remembering the years of want as a boy and living in Milwaukee as a rookie. In 1955, Hank and Barbara Aaron lived in a three-room apartment on 29th Street in Milwaukee. Their tiny living room held two pieces of furniture: a small, imitation leather easy chair and a portable television set which worked on a part-time basis. "Our place was so small, we couldn't even get a couch in the living room" he said. "I was getting paid the six thousand dollar minimum as a rookie and some of my relatives were carried away because I was in the big leagues. They ran up some bills to my account and I had a hell of a time making ends meet."

With the new contract, Aaron could easily make ends meet, and an investment business he and Billy Bruton had begun years before was rapidly expanding. The Aaron-Bruton Company owned four apartment buildings in central Milwaukee which accepted only long-term leases. In addition, Aaron bought four houses and a 1700-acre farming tract in Mobile, along with a grocery store for his parents.

So he want to Atlanta in April a financially comfortable man. The city officially welcomed the club with a motorcade that was viewed by a quarter-million Atlantans. A 14-man police motorcycle escort was necessary to keep order. One car, however, was mobbed. The one in which Hank Aaron was riding. Atlanta Mayor Ivan Allen called the day "an historic occasion . . . the happiest day Atlanta's had since we got rid of General Sherman."

If Aaron wasn't ecstatic about the Braves' move south, he was resigned to it, and after the motorcade ended, he denied he had said he would not play in the south.

"I said it would be hard to leave Milwaukee . . . but I never said I wouldn't move down here. That's just one of the many stories some sports writers have twisted. We saw some truly lovely houses here. If I don't move my family, I might as well join the Army. That would be crazy. I couldn't stand being away from them so long."

So the Aarons moved to Atlanta to a previously segregated neighborhood. There were no major incidents, although after weeks of playing with the Aaron kids without problem or fanfare, most white children in the neighborhood suddenly were no longer allowed to visit the Aaron home.

When the 1966 season began, Aaron established his goals. "I want to hit forty-five home runs. Before I'm through, I should be able to hit five hundred (he and Mathews went into the season with eight hundred and three, a major-league record for teammates). Then, although it's a big order, I'd like to get three thousand hits before my career's over. I'm past the two thousand mark now.

"I think this park in Atlanta is fair for hitters and for pitchers. I believe I'll be able to hit home runs here OK."

The Braves' move climaxed a three-year search by Atlanta leaders for a major-league team. The Braves—who would make $991,885 in 1966—lost $1,517,061 their final year in Milwaukee. When the season began (the Braves drew 50,671 fans to a night opener) the lawsuit brought by Milwaukee fans had reached the Wisconsin Supreme Court. There it died, the court ruling the move was legal. The U.S. Supreme Court then refused to hear an appeal and the matter was settled.

Unsettled were the Braves. They slipped below the .500 level on May 10th, 1966 and never really were a factor in the National League pennant race. Manager Bobby Bragan had too few pluses. Four pitchers in the Brave rotation suffered arm miseries during the campaign, Wade Blasingame, Denny Lemaster, Don Schwall and Joey Jay. The club having been in seventh or eighth place much of the summer, general manager John McHale fired Bragan on August 9th, replacing him with coach Billy Hitchcock. Bragan had made several enemies on the club, in particular, Eddie Mathews, Lemaster, and Lew Burdette, and aside from Aaron and a few other players he was not missed.

As often occurs, following Bragan's firing the Braves

immediately turned the season around. Hitchcock returned the aging Mathews to third base and Atlanta streaked down the homestretch, winning 19 of its last 21 games to finish fifth, a respectable 10 games behind the pennant-winning Los Angeles Dodgers.

The season had both ups and downs for Hank Aaron. He had minor surgery on an ankle in the spring and started slowly, his average never recovering its normal range. He hit .279, the first time in six years he had failed to breach the .300 level. Conversely he led the league with 44 home runs, the third time he had reached that figure, and 127 RBIs. He also stole 21 bases in 24 attempts, the highest percentage in baseball. And he was finally being accorded respect. If he was not considered a full-blown superstar, he was thought of, at least, as super.

"He's the last guy in the league I want to see coming to the plate," said the game's premier pitcher, Los Angeles' Sandy Koufax. "You just don't get away with a mistake to Henry Aaron."

Enough mistakes had been made so that when the 1966 season closed, Henry Aaron had hit 442 home run, No. 400 coming the first week in the seaon off a fastball thrown by Philadelphia's Bo Belinsky. Later Aaron would remember realizing that he could wind up one of the game's finest home run hitters, perhaps even closing his career with as many as 600. It was at this stage that he also realized he could recall each of his home runs. Three years before, he had tagged Ron Perranoski for No. 303 in a game in Los Angeles. In 1966, a reporter casually reminded him of the game. "Yeah, it was a fastball, high and away. It was the first pitch and I guess I was looking for it. I figured he'd try to set me up for his sinker."

Bobby Bragan, still running the club that day, nodded. A few years before he had ordered Pittsburgh pitcher Vernon Law to start Aaron out with a knuckleball.

"Let's see what he can do with that," Bragan told Law. What Aaron did was deposit it in a tree behind the left-field wall at Forbes Field. "I figured he'd try to fool me at first with the knuckleball," Aaron told Bragan.

The 1966 season had held its share of surprises for Aaron. As late as June 15th, he was ahead of the 1961 home-run pace followed by Roger Maris when he hit 61. The short-lived chase of Maris provided Aaron with a slight understanding of the pressures that he would later come to appreciate.

"They were trying to win a pennant and he was bugged a lot," Aaron said of the pressure which Maris had to endure. "I talked to guys on the Yankees then and they said he couldn't even eat breakfast without someone waking him up to do it."

Bragan was asked if such pressure would effect the normally imperturbable Aaron. "Nah... it wouldn't bother him. He's as stable as any ballplayer in the business. The thing that makes him so great is that he does everything so easy... without frills."

When Maris' record began outdistancing him, Aaron took it with his usual aplomb. "If you go up there looking for homers, you don't hit them. I was just fortunate for a while. Everything I hit hard went out of the park."

Being fortunate had nothing to do with it, thought Leo Durocher. If the public generally ignored Aaron, the Chicago Cubs' manager did not.

"He's the best righthanded hitter since Hornsby," the Lip said. "He's the toughest out in the game now. I remember one game... I forget who was pitching, but he threw Aaron a changeup. Henry hit it eighty-four feet over the fence in left field. Now he figures he better not throw that again the next time, so he jams Aaron with a fastball. Aaron hits it on a line over the right field fence, about four inches inside the foul pole."

Durocher went on almost poetically about Henry

Aaron the ballplayer. In days to come, the Loquacious One would never tire of talking about "Bad Henry... the best hitter in baseball."

Still, the public yawned. When 1966 ended, no less an authority than Ted Wiliams said, "Aaron is one of the all-time greats." The public by and large nodded drowsily, and quickly forgot Williams' remark and Aaron's accomplishments.

In fact, in 1966, Aaron derived less public attention than his wife did when she was arrested by police outside Atlanta Stadium one night in August after police charged her with creating a disturbance.

There were varying opinions on what had happened, but Barbara Aaron was charged with "disorderly conduct, cursing and failure to obey an officer's signal." An Atlanta patrolman, L. W. Bedgood, said Mrs. Aaron wouldn't move her car from a lot, as he had directed. Barbara Aaron said traffic prevented her from moving the car and that Bedgood had pointed his revolver at her and kept calling her "woman." Bedgood said he had merely placed his hand on the butt of his pistol. Five witnesses allegedly testified Bedgood had waved the pistol and said, "I'll blow your damn brains out, nigger."

"My wife said the worst word she used was damn," Aaron said.

Bedgood and two other policemen involved in work at the stadium were suspended but later reinstated, and all charges were dropped. The incident got Aaron more publicity than his on-the-field exploits.

And though Henry Aaron would in the next three season mount assaults on some of the game's most-cherished accomplishments, he would remain ignored.

10

The Avis Approach

Hank Aaron walks into a Cincinnati hotel the day before an All-Star Game. He cannot remember an All-Star Game in which he has not been a performer. He asks a reservations clerk for his room. The clerk checks the list. "Sorry," he says, "but we have nothing in your name. Hank Aaron? Who are you with, Mr. Aaron?"

A burglar breaks into the Houston home of Astro executive Tal Smith. On the mantlepiece in a glass case are two autographed baseballs. The thief takes the ball signed by Hank Aaron; leaves the ball signed by Willie Mays. Told about the burglary, Hank Aaron smiles wistfully. "All that proves is the guy couldn't read."

The Atlanta Braves publish a yearbook with Hank Aaron's picture on the cover. Because of the shading in the picture, Aaron appears faceless. Ironically, the headline above the picture silently screams a truth: "Hello, Meet No. 3011-1997-636." The numbers, relating to Aaron's batting accomplishments as of late 1971, are

President Lyndon B. Johnson welcomes a member of his Council on Physical Fitness in 1967.

The All-Star Game in Washington in 1969 occasioned an invitation to meet with President Nixon.

meant to introduce a man who should need no introduction. Fans continually call the Braves office, confused by the yearbook's cover.

It is a hot Sunday afternoon in Atlanta. The Braves are playing Cincinnati. Early in the game, Atlanta catcher Bob Tillman lifts a towering fly ball that drifts towards the seats running parallel with the right-field foul line. Cincinnati rightfielder Pete Rose dashes madly in pursuit of the ball. His hat falls off, his stubby legs pump wildly like pistons gone mad. Reaching the railing, he lunges and stabs at the ball, misses, and in the last milli-second before disaster, somehow goes up and over the fence. The crowd roars wildly for Charlie Hustle. That, the fans assure one another, is, by God, what makes baseball the national pastime.

Later in the same game, another fly ball is lifted into the same area under like circumstance. Hank Aaron lopes in pursuit. He does not sprint, but rather seems to glide effortlessly, as if on ice. Reaching the railing, he steadies himself, judges the flight of the ball, leans over the fence and makes a routine catch. Nine paying customers yawn and decide to go to the john.

So, because he never had Mays' idiosyncrasies or Clemente's fire or Mantle's injuries, Aaron lived perpetually in baseball's shadows with his accomplishments and his truly incredible consistency. And, despite the talent that ran on like a lava flow, he would remain unsung through the rest of the 1960s.

He was Hank Aaron, the almost-superstar. Baseball's Invisible Man. He threw no tantrums, uttered no shrill words, fought no opponents, Never quite the artist; ever the master craftsman. Striding through the summers alone, lacking the charisma that separates a Ruth from a Gehrig, a Chamberlain from a Russell. And in the years from 1967 through 1969, the world continued to pretty much disregard Hank Aaron, whose cross was that no matter the breadth of his accomplishments, he never even once was a shooting star streaking across the game's heavens.

No one quite understood why—why time had not brought fame. Perhaps because he never quite dominated the National League at bat, although he led it in home runs and RBIs four times and average twice. Atlanta Braves' official Lee Walburn was as puzzled by Aaron's nonentity as anyone. "It's almost like he was a creature out of history, a man known more by figures than by his face, as opposed to a Joe Namath, who would be known on any street corner in the country yet who has reached nowhere near the accomplishments Hank has."

Pontificating in *The Sporting News,* publisher C. C. Johnson Spink wrote, "Aaron will not leave baseball as a nonentity, but his press clippings are sparse in relation to his status as one of the great hitters in baseball history."

In time, Aaron came to ignore his lack of attention, hiding behind statements like: "I want to be remembered as just plain Hank Aaron." It was left to his teammates to delve into the reasons for the neglect of Henry Aaron.

"The funny thing about Henry Aaron is that you're not going to be impressed with him at first sight," Billy Bruton said. "I know I wasn't. You have to see him every day to appreciate him. He just isn't very colorful. He makes it all look so easy. When he first joined the Braves, we'd hold our breath every time a fly ball went in his direction. It was the way he went after a ball, like he was never going to get there. But after we saw him awhile and saw the kinds of things he could do, we quit worrying."

Thought Brave infielder Clete Boyer, "He just makes this game look so easy . . . he's a complete player, a large cut above all the rest of us. He always has complete control of himself. I've seen him hit two home runs and then come in the clubhouse and sit down in front of his stall and say nothing about it. He can go 0-for-4 and act the same way. His life is baseball, and he loves it."

For some years, Aaron activated a series of defense mechanisms to ward off the disappointment he felt at being unappreciated by the press as well as the general public. Of course, there were reasons for his remaining the game's most unknown superstar.

He had always played in out-of-the-way cities. The New York press could, he thought, make a celebrity out of a harmonica player like Phil Linz. "If I had played in New York, I believe I would've made two million dollars," he said. "I've never had the advantage of playing in a city where there were more than two newspapers. Everyone knows stuff like 'Say, Hey.' Guys who play in New York get great publicity."

But primary to the inattention he received was his personality, his modus operandi on the field and off. He was a private person. "I've always been that way . . . always been a loner." Because he took the game seriously, he went about it with all the flamboyance of a tax accountant. "I never smile when I have a bat in my hands. That's when you've got to be serious. When I get out on the field, nothing's a joke to me. I don't feel I should walk around with a smile on my face.

"I'm kind of reserved, hard to get close to. I've never been a big talker and maybe if I'd had the TV and newspaper guys around me, I'd have said things I would have regretted later."

In short, he played and lived, at least as far as the public ever knew, dispassionately. Avoiding controversy —"I don't let anything distract me from the game"—as he avoided unorthodox clothing or speech habits. "That's my style," he would shrug.

But as the 1960s wound down, that style palled. "When they start naming players, they say 'Mays-Aaron' or 'Mantle-Aaron'. It's never 'Aaron-Mays' or 'Aaron-Mantle'. I was a lost cause in Milwaukee. I was always in the shadows of the big boys—Mathews, Spahn, Burdette—I think people there were just waiting for me to fall on my face. I knew the other guys were important . . . but Henry Aaron was important too."

And, as it had earlier for Avis, being second worked wonders for Hank Aaron. It fired in him a desire to out-reach his anonymity, to challenge Olympian heights. "I'm always second—always have been. I guess that's given me extra incentive. When you're second-best, you try harder in order to be first.

"You get tired of being taken for granted."

So what do you do when your accomplishments so outdistance your fame as to have the situation become a *cause célèbre?* How does one go about pulling fame down around his shoulders?

How about scaling the very highest peak of them all, thought Hank Aaron. How about going for the one standard that guaranteed immortality? How about making an Avis out of, well, how about Babe Ruth?

The idea evolved slowly as Aaron continued to pile up the home runs in the late 1960s. Certainly he had been spoken of as a challenger to Ruth's career home run record. But only in light conversation, the way it must have been speculated that, perhaps, in the distant future, there would come a speedster to better Cobb's stolen-base records. No, in the late 1960s, if Ruth had a bonafide challenger it was thought to be Mays or Harmon Kille-brew. The failure to hear his name added to any such list irritated—and perhaps goaded—Aaron.

So in 1967, he took stock of his chances to surpass the great Ruth. Going into the season he had whacked 442 home runs. At 33 years of age, he was setting a pace too slow to even approach Ruth. He searched his records. The numbers were good, very good. But, he knew, not good enough to muster serious challenge to Ruth.

"Second best," Aaron would say later, a trace of sarcasm in his voice. "Like they said Killebrew had a chance. And Mays. And, oh yeah, maybe Aaron." Maybe Aaron. Pride burned a hole in his psyche. "I hadn't really accomplished anything. I felt disappointed in myself. I decided I had to keep going."

So, Hank Aaron kept going, now in silent pursuit of the Babe. Before the 1967 season began, he made a decision. Age was slowing his bat ever so slightly, so he lowered it and pulled his hands in closer to his body "to get to the ball a little quicker." The target had become No. 715, although not publicly. "Seven-fourteen," he laughed one day before the year began. "I don't think about that. All I care about is the next one."

That was, of course, a lie. Pride made Aaron think about it. And there were other factors. In 1967, Aaron was, more than ever before, expected to hit home runs. The Braves had traded Eddie Mathews and his 493 career home runs to Houston and there was some slack to be taken up. "We were more than teammates," a shocked Aaron said. "He was the only guy I ever saw that I could communicate with. I had ideas and he had ideas, and we talked about them. And the competition between us made both of us better ballplayers."

The absence of Mathews made Hank Aaron the Braves' Main Man. And Main Men get the top dollar. In February, Aaron and Atlanta president Bill Bartholomay went into a meeting to discuss contract. When they came out, Aaron was the first Brave to ever receive a $100,000 contract, having signed for two years. "I went for the works, and I got what I wanted," Aaron said.

What Aaron wanted in 1967 was the long ball, and with Mathews gone he reached for it more than ever. "True," he agreed he was swinging more for distance, "but it also has to do with the ballpark you're playing in. The ball is so alive in Atlanta that I can hit it out almost any time I get good wood on it. So I'm trying more for the long ball."

He got it, hitting 39 home runs and thus becoming the lone saving grace for a Brave club that had reached rock bottom. It was, at least personally, Aaron's longest season. A spiritless aggregate, Atlanta finished seventh, failing to play .500 baseball for the first time in 15 years. At mid-season, Aaron and Rico Carty caused a further dissolution of team morale by engaging in a fight aboard a flight from Houston to Los Angeles. Apparently it was triggered by jealousy. Aaron had ceased to become Carty's patron over the years, the fiery Dominican's temper tiresome to a quiet man. Carty resented the fact that Aaron's status had earned him the right to room by himself on the road, a privilege accorded to many outstanding veterans.

Aaron and infielder Mike de la Hoz were chatting when the slumping Carty, who had hit .326 the year before but had fallen to .260 by mid-June, interrupted them, referring to Aaron, who was leading the league in home runs and RBIs at that point, as "a black bastard."

Aaron swung immediately, although with far less accuracy than he usually brought to the curve ball. His right fist missed Carty, struck pitcher Pat Jarvis a glancing blow and smashed into the overhead rack. Carty counterpunched and it took pitchers Tony Cloninger and Clay Carroll and outfielder Gary Geiger to restrain Aaron.

"Henry was boiling . . . I never saw him like that," traveling secretary Don Davidson said. The incident was not untypical of the Braves. Shortstop Johnny Logan and pitcher Vern Bickford had engaged in a fight in front of a hotel a few years before, and during another season, Earl Torgeson and Jim Russell had gotten into a public brawl. But it was indicative of the Brave mood and came just a few days after manager Billy Hitchcock had fined six Braves, including Aaron, for missing a bed check.

"It was a matter of pride," Aaron said amid speculation that Carty would be traded. "That's one thing I don't take. If it happens again, I'll hit him again. I'm not afraid of him, the only thing he could do is whip my tail, if it comes to that."

In a prelude to a controversy that would bloom with interesting consequences two years later, Aaron and Atlanta announcer Milo Hamilton became embroiled in a feud triggered by Hamilton's reference to Pittsburgh's Roberto Clemente as the game's finest right fielder.

"This was my longest, most frustrating season," Aaron lashed out at the conclusion of the 1967 campaign, at which time Hitchcock was fired. "The morale was so low ... some of the guys gave up two months ago. I can't understand things like that. I don't want to sound like I'm criticizing my teammates, but I can't understand guys playing just to get the season over.

"I'm 34 ... I'd like to play for a pennant winner, a World Series team again. There's nothing like that pride you feel on a team that's going all out, giving everything, everyday."

The 1968 season began on a positive note. Disgusted by the apathy the Braves had demonstrated the previous season, Aaron took more of a leadership role in the spring. "This is the place to start getting serious," he said at the West Palm Beach training site. "Right here is where you build your spirit." Paul Richards, however, wasn't enamored of the Aaron spirit. A crusty disciplinarian who went from month to month without being observed smiling, Richards had brought in a good, old, down-home country boy, Luman Harris, to replace Hitchcock, and he was determined that no team of his would be undisciplined, On or off the field.

In June, perhaps disgruntled by a batting average hovering in the low .200 range, Aaron ripped baseball for racial prejudice, saying he seriously doubted he would ever have the opportunity to manage in the majors. Richards immediately bridled. "He is welcome to his opinion," Richards snapped, "but baseball has done more for the Negro race than all the crusaders and politicians you can name. When a Negro player comes along who is qualified, he'll get his chance. Furthermore, I think Henry Aaron ought to be pointing out the advantages of baseball, not its disadvantages. I can't help but wondering what he'd be doing without baseball."

Aaron fired back. "All baseball has done for me? What about all I've done for baseball." A coolness developed between them that existed until Richards left the organization several years later.

Aaron had other problems in 1968, failing to get untracked at the plate until after the all-star break, when despite his .236 average he was named to the team. But his slump was, if not broken, cracked on July 14th.

In a home game against San Francisco, Giant lefty Mike McCormick gave up singles to Felipe Alou and Felix Millan, and then hung a curveball in Hank Aaron's eyes.

The ball left the park at the 400-foot mark and slammed against a message board, allowing it to be retrieved and presented to its author. When Aaron crossed the plate, a half-dozen teammates and club president Bill Bartholomay were there to meet him. As he stepped on the plate, Aaron told his boss, "I'm sorry you had to wait so long, Bill."

No. 500 had been struck and Bad Henry had become only the eighth player in the game's long history to have reached that exalted plateau. Applause from 34,238 fans, largest crowd of the year, swelled and rolled across the playing surface to burst in waves against the outfield walls. "The fans here are so nice . . . I never had an ovation like that."

Later in the Brave clubhouse, Aaron held the ball gingerly, squeezing it occasionally as he spoke with writers. "My biggest home run? This one. Other than this one, the one I hit that won the pennant in 1957. When I hit this one, it was like 1957 and all my teammates came out to shake my hand. And somehow it means more hitting it off a Cy Young Award pitcher like Mike."

Ironically, Herbert Aaron had come to Atlanta from Mobile for the occasion, only to leave town that morning. "After I got within one of 500, I called home and asked my mother and father to come down. Mother was sick, but my Dad came. Three days he was here and I couldn't even come close to getting it for him. He said when he left, 'You'll get it tonight.' "

The home run was Aaron's 2700th career hit but it failed to generate great excitement, and it was not until sometime later that it was discovered that Aaron was 11 home runs ahead of Ruth at the same age. Several baseball experts, however, did predict Aaron would reach the 600 mark before he retired.

On the night of August 24th, outside the door to the Atlanta clubhouse, a small woman stood crying softly. "I was just remembering . . . just remembering how Ben would come home from the ballpark and say 'Mary, that Aaron is going to be some great ballplayer,' " Mary Geraghty said. She had come to Atlanta for Hank Aaron Night, along with the Aaron family and many of his former teammates.

A crowd of 31,246 turned out to see Aaron given dozens of gifts, including a new car and a diamond ring. When it came time for him to speak, Aaron said chokingly into the microphone, "Above all, I thank God for giving me the talent to play."

In the clubhouse earlier, he had posed for pictures with his fellow Mobilean, Satchel Paige. "I'm glad I was lucky enough to come along at the right time," Aaron said.

143

Aware that fate had dealt him out of a similar moment in the sun, Paige was uncommonly restrained until a photographer posed him with Aaron and urged, "C'mon, smile at the best-looking man in the world." Paige suddenly brightened and craned his neck, "I'se tryin' to see myself."

Aaron repaid the crowd that night as best he could, with a long home run. "I kind of felt obligated," he laughed.

But in 1968, there was little else that amused Aaron. He finished the year with a four-year low in home runs, 29, and his 86 RBIs were fewer than he had produced in 15 summers. And the Braves ended up fifth. In step with his other woes, the Aarons' home burned to the ground in August, destroying all but a few of the many trophies he had accumulated over the years.

Yet when a reporter asked him about the losses, he said, "Our poodle was killed and that was pretty tough on the kids. When the firemen got in the house, the dog was still in his basket."

During the winter, Aaron was hired as an evening sportscaster by Atlanta station WQXI, providing a delicious irony of sorts considering it was his feud with Braves' announcer Milo Hamilton that triggered a public announcement which snatched the baseball public by the throat.

Hamilton owns, not necessarily in their order of importance, a large, loyal following of listeners throughout the South; a shocking pink embroidered cowboy hat; an impressive collection of baseball statistics; vocal cords which should be bronzed when he has no further need of them, and an ego with which Howard Cosell would be comfortable. "When Milo rents the honeymoon suite," says an Atlanta writer "he stays in it alone."

Referred to, not always kindly, as "The Mouth of the South," Hamilton is called by no less authority than veteran Atlanta sports editor Jesse Outlar "a house man." Which is a writer or broadcaster with the tendency to overlook any and all failings of the team which he is covering. Which definition undoubtedly would normally include Hamilton.

But early in the 1969 season Hamilton became, for the first time in his career, publicly critical of the Braves, although the evidence seems to indicate critical might be too strong a word. In any case, he managed to antagonize Aaron, who had been told by listeners that Hamilton didn't seem overly enthused in describing Aaron's heroics.

"You want a story?" Aaron asked Atlanta *Journal* baseball writer Wilt Browning one night. "Sure," said Browning.

"I'd like to play under a different atmosphere," Aaron told the stunned writer. "I want the Braves to get Hamilton off my back. I'm just not going to continue to be chewed up on the radio. All those years I played in the shadow of Spahn and Mathews and Burdette. But I don't have to play in anybody's shadow now. I've been abused from every angle and I've lived with it, but not anymore."

Then came the bombshell, the thought of which still brings a professional gleam to the eyes of the normally unexcitable Browning. "I would like seriously to go for Babe Ruth's home run record. I think I could do it—and that's the first time I've ever confessed that.

"But I'm not going to live under this situation four or five more years."

Editorialized the Atlanta *Journal*: "How many home runs did Hamilton hit last year?"

A meeting between the combatants and Braves' president Bill Bartholomay provided an immediate truce and so Hank Aaron began, at least publicly, the quest of Ruth. History has recorded one further piece of irony: Hamilton has announced all of Aaron's home runs from that day forward, his broadcasting partner Ernie Johnson always off-mike each time Aaron appears at the plate.

Later, Aaron would say of the incident, "I've never been so embarrassed in my life."

For a change, the Braves had nothing to be embarrassed about as they battled Cincinnati and San Francisco throughout the summer of 1969 for the lead in the National League West.

Aaron continued to hammer the ball, hitting No. 521 on June 21st against Chicago to tie Ted Williams for fifth on the all-time list. On his next at-bat, Chicago righthander Dick Selma twice knocked Aaron down with pitches. Aaron moved toward the man and told Selma he was "bush." After the game the Brave star ripped Cub manager Leo Durocher.

"He ordered Selma to throw at my legs. They're about all I have left now. I didn't wait this long to get hit and hurt."

Aaron was correct; it was too late to intimidate him. At midyear he was hitting .340 and had 17 home runs, which prompted the Global League, a new circuit just getting organized, to offer him a half-million dollars to jump leagues.

The Braves undoubtedly would've offered him that sum to stay had it been necessary. Getting brilliant pitching from kunckleballers Phil Niekro, who would win 23 games, and reliever Hoyt Wilhelm, the Braves hung tough in a pennant chase so intense that in one September day, the Braves held first place in the morning; Cincinnati in the afternoon, and San Francisco at night.

But down the stretch, the Braves gradually pried the pennant from the hands of both San Francisco and Cincinnati, winning 27 of their last 37 games and clinching the pennant September 30 with a 4-2 win in Cincinnati.

But as hot as they were in the closing days of the season, the Braves fell to the New York Mets in three straight games in the National League playoffs despite three home runs by Aaron during the series.

Still, the 1969 season had been a huge success for both the Braves, who had their best season in 11 years, and Aaron, whose 44 home runs gave him a career total of 552.

Now there were only three objectives he truly cherished: Ruth's record, his 3,000th hit, and general recognition that it was both unjust and inaccurate to place Bad Henry Aaron second to anyone.

Two of those objectives would be reached in 1970.

11

Hank's Mental Bank

Suddenly in the spring of 1970, after 17 splendid summers, Henry Aaron became an overnight sensation, a publicly certified marvel. However, he would not entirely surrender the cloak of obscurity he had worn for so long. Richard Nixon would continue to address his Christmas card to "Frank" Aaron, and later, on the occasion of a truly historic home run, the White House would send a wire of congratulations to, of all places, the Milwaukee Boosters Club.

But in the opening weeks of the 1970 baseball season, it was undeniable that a vast subconscious wrong was in the process of being righted; that the American public had awakened to the exploits of the man called Hammer. In Montreal's Jarry Park, he was being accorded standing ovations each time his name was announced—in French. Sportswriters stumbled over one another in seeking to interview Aaron, aware at last that he was running hard on the heels of two tremendous baseball records at the same instant: 3,000 hits and the home run record of Babe Whozits.

"I feel it now, and hear it," said Atlanta third baseman Clete Boyer. "Maybe the fact that he's colored has hurt him in getting publicity, but maybe the fact that he's colored has helped him to understand people more than any other player I've ever known."

Perhaps, more than for any other single reason, consistency was the keynote to increased interest in Aaron. In a game that demands it of its genuine heroes, no player of his era played the game with such sustained excellence. In an average season, Aaron would hit .314, crank out 34 home runs, drive in 108, steal 14 bases, and in 592 appearances at the plate, reach base safely 243 times.

The players had held this purposeful, deliberate craftsman in awe for years, and in 1970 something of what they felt had begun to be perceived by the public. "The applause for him is amazing now," said Aaron's brother-in-law, Bill Lucas.

"The slights made me fight that much harder," said Aaron, "but, really, the lack of attention didn't bother me one bit. I'll tell you why. First off, who knows how successful I would've been with a lot of added attention and pressure? Look at Roger Maris. He was almost driven nuts by the pressure. And attention doesn't really matter that much in the end. It may sound like a cliché, but the only important thing is whether you win. Last year, even though my statistics were good and we won the Western Division, I felt miserable at the end of the year because we didn't win the pennant and I knew we should have."

Two weeks before spring training began, Aaron started girding himself for the chase of hit No. 3,000 and Babe Ruth by negotiating another record contract. Club president Bill Bartholomay made an offer, Aaron "told him what I was asking." Bartholomay scratched his head for a moment and stuck out his hand. The two-year, $250,000 contract was signed. "I wanted two years because everywhere I go, people keep asking me if I'm going to retire and now I won't have to answer that one for awhile."

During spring training, Aaron hit an even .500 in 42 at-bats while tutoring Ralph Garr, a rookie being groomed as his eventual successor. "I don't think I've ever seen Hank swing the bat better," Braves' manager Luman Harris said the final week of spring training. "It shouldn't take him long to get that three-thousandth hit."

It didn't. No. 3,000 came on Sunday, May 18th in Cincinnati. The night before, the phone in Aaron's room rang incessantly until 3 a.m., when he told the telephone operator not to put through any more calls. At 9 a.m., he ate a small breakfast, saying "I'm a little bit nervous about all of this." Before the Atlanta team bus left for Cincinnati's Crosley Field at 10:45, the Reds' Pete Rose came by the Braves' hotel to laughingly inform Aaron that if he got ahold of Aaron's 3,000th hit, he was "going to throw it out of the park so you can't have a souvenir."

On the bus to the ballpark, none of the Braves mentioned Aaron's pending meeting with a destiny only eight other players in history had known. The most recent one, Stan Musial, arrived at the Cincinnati airport at 10:58 and stopped to get his shoes shined. "Aaron only needs one more for 3,000," the shoeshine boy informed The Man, who had come to Cincinnati for the event.

At noon, Ernie Banks called Aaron in the Atlanta clubhouse and a moment later Aaron stroked batting practice pitcher Jim Busby's first effort off the scoreboard.

At 12:45, traveling secretary Donald Davidson signed a $200 check to be given to the fan who caught Aaron's 3,000th hit should it leave the park, and equipment man Mark Gladulich stationed himself beyond the left field fence to make certain the ball would be returned in that eventuality.

Just before the first game of the doubleheader began,

Reds' lefthander Jim Merritt told a writer, "He's going to have to earn it. But he knows I'll throw him strikes. I'm pulling for him."

The historical hit did not come off Merritt, who beat the Braves, 5-1, and retired Aaron on two groundouts, a long fly to dead center and a strikeout. But at precisely 4:05 p.m., Aaron hit a Wayne Simpson fastball back through the middle. Reds' shortstop Woody Woodward roamed deep behind the bag and made the play, but had no chance to get Aaron and wisely held the ball.

Musial and Bartholomay hopped the box-seat railing and ran out to first base. Musial presented the ball to Aaron with a huge grin. "Welcome to the club." After 16 years, 19,566 at-bats and 2,460 games, Hank Aaron had climbed a mountain that had defeated, among others, Babe Ruth, Ted Williams, Rogers Hornsby, Lou Gehrig, Joe DiMaggio, Mel Ott and Mickey Mantle.

The accolades gushed, but no one put it better than Atlanta's Joe Torre: "That old saying's true . . . he belongs in a higher league."

Alas, the Braves did not, falling 10 games under .500 and finishing a dismal fifth in the National League West. Even Aaron's brilliant start—he had 16 home runs the first week in May—didn't help. But, as usual, while the Braves were plummeting, Henry Aaron steadfastly did his thing. He hit .298 with 38 home run and 118 RBIs and when the 1970 season ended with him becoming the first man in baseball history to have combined 500 home runs and 3,000 hits, two of the goals he had sought in the spring had been achieved.

Recognition and the 3,000th hit had come; left was the Babe's lofty mark. He had, assuming the average home run travels at least 340 feet, more than 37 miles of them, and with 592 on the books, Ruth's record hoved into sight.

The 3,000 Club: Stan Musial, Willie Mays and Aaron, each a 3,000-hit man, are honored by the St. Louis Baseball Writers Association in 1971.

"This year and the next are the critical ones for me if I'm going to catch Ruth," he said. "I would almost have to have fifty a year in one of the two seasons. I'm going to just hang on and hit one once in awhile.

"Catching Ruth would be a thrill, but getting three-thousand hits was more important because it shows consistency. People keep wanting to know if I will be around long enough to break Ruth's record. I don't know. I do know I will not hang on just for the sake of hanging on, picking up twelve one year, maybe twenty the next. I have too much respect for baseball to do that."

The year 1971 was, as Aaron had predicted, critical. But for reasons other than his pursuit of Ruth. After 18 years of marriage, Hank and Barbara Aaron agreed to a quiet, "friendly divorce" that occurred months before the public became aware of it. Friends agree their parting was as amicable as possible: Two different personalities going their separate ways.

"It was really something to go through," Aaron said, "especially with four kids involved. It was a terrible adjustment for me. I was depressed. I spent a great deal of time alone. I threw myself into baseball to get my mind off it, but . . . it took a long time for me to get back on the right track. How do you explain it to four children who love both parents? Things happen and you don't know why they happen, and the more they happen, the further apart you get. Things kids wouldn't understand."

A proud, solicitous father, Aaron worried of the effect the divorce would have on his children: Gaile, 20, a student at Fisk University in Nashville; Hank Jr., 17; Larry, 16, and Dorinda, 12. But he had long been concerned for his children and made every effort to keep their lives as private as his own.

Of Hank Jr., he said, "Maybe I should've named him John or Harry . . . anything but Hank Jr. It might be too much of a burden on him, and that would be very unfair."

When an Atlanta reporter wanted to interview Larry —like his older brother a fine high school football player —Aaron would not hear of it. "A sixteen-year-old boy, what can he say? I just want him to play football and study, and not be embarrassed in front of his teammates."

Following his divorce, Aaron moved from the rambling five-bedroom home in the Southwest Atlanta neighborhood that he and his family had integrated, but which in time had become all-black, and moved to a five-room high rise apartment on Piedmont Avenue, from which he can see the stadium lights.

He continued ever the loner, eating his meals at Leb's, a kosher restaurant featuring the shrimp curry and creole dishes he favors over steak, and a tiny diner in an Atlanta ghetto where the specialties of the house are baked chicken and gumbo.

"Henry has successfully guarded his private life," says a friend.

Media people continued to be dismayed at failing to crack the shield Aaron had thrown up around himself. He dressed expensively but conservatively—"I don't look at the price tag; if I like something, I buy it"—and lived much the same way.

"Hank's idea of a big night out is dinner at a Polynesian restaurant," laughs a friend.

One reporter from a national magazine agreed. "The more you dig into him, the more you get the impression of a bland fellow with a talent for baseball."

Certainly in 1971, no one could deny Aaron's talent. While the Braves were staggering along as usual in the wake of mediocrity—they would finish third in the NL West at 82-80—Aaron was enjoying, at the advanced age of 37, perhaps his finest season ever.

Even before it began, Las Vegas gambler Jimmy (the Greek) Snyder had made him "even money" to catch Ruth, but Aaron didn't quite agree with the odds. "If all goes well, and I stay healthy, I think my chances are better than even," he said in spring training.

But, if he was enjoying the spotlight, he sought to share it with Willie Mays and Ruth. "I think Willie has a good chance if he wants to hang around long enough," said Aaron, who would in time become a bit disenchanted with the aging San Francisco star. "And I don't think anyone could ever take Ruth's place. Even if he was passed, he'd still be looked upon as the greatest home run hitter ever."

And what of Bad Henry Aaron? "I think that it would be a hell of a thing if I could break the record," Aaron smiled.

On April 27 that became a very distinct possibility. Earlier that morning, as the sun peeked over a hill and let its rays flicker into Toulminville, Estella Aaron bustled about her house with unusual good cheer. "This is the day," she called a premonition to her husband and then went to the telephone to relay the thought to Hank Aaron.

San Francisco pitcher Gaylord Perry held no such premonition. "If he gets it off me, he's going to earn it," the bony righthander observed, history failing to record if he licked his lips when he made the statement.

Aaron arrived at Atlanta Stadium around 4 p.m., read his mail, some of it containing the hate that would spew forth by the volume later, and relaxed in a whirlpool bath trying to shake a case of the flu which had idled him for two days.

When the game began, Aaron still felt a bit drained, and approached the plate slowly in the third inning after Ralph Garr had singled. Ignoring his favorite pitch, the moisture content of which has been a favorite baseball topic for years, Perry tried to jam Aaron with a high, tight fastball.

Aaron hit it on a flat line and the 13,494 fans at Atlanta Stadium wearing "I was There" cards went bananas. Home Run No. 600, carrying almost no trajectory, screamed against the left field wall and now three men— Ruth, Mays, Aaron—belonged to baseball's most exclusive club.

Plate umpire Shag Crawford sidled up to Aaron later and said, "When you look back on this twenty years from now, remember ol' Shag was behind the plate."

When Aaron replaced an injured Orlando Cepeda at first base late in the game, Mays came by to shake his hand. "If you think the fans got shook up tonight, tell 'em to stick around because he's not through rockin' this place yet," said Mays, whose career lead over Aaron had dwindled to 33 home runs.

In the clubhouse after San Francisco had won the game, ironically on a hit by Mays, Aaron was surrounded by reporters eagerly awaiting post-game comments equal to the momentous occasion. As usual, they were disappointed. Henry Aaron remained Henry Aaron, speaking in quiet, heartfelt banalities.

Of No. 714, he said "That's a long way off. I'll just try to get one home run at a time." And of the excitement he felt, "I got a bigger thrill from my three-thousandth hit." And of the national press which had followed Mays for days waiting for No. 600 but now was nowhere in sight, "They never paid much attention to me for years . . . so I'm glad they're not here now."

When he spoke of the home run in abstract terms, even the writers close to him blanched. "When they talk about Hank Aaron, I just want them to say, 'He was a good hitter.' I don't want to be known as a home run hitter.

I'm not a home run hitter . . . I like to look at myself as a complete ballplayer.

"Just call me a hitter."

But that would not do; would be like calling Raquel Welch just a movie star, the Stradivariius just a musical instrument.

To watch him enter the clubhouse is to know he is far more than a hitter. Seated in front of his locker—an open booth perhaps five feet wide—he is a presence, and looking at him you are reminded of Bill Russell's theory that there are no superior athletes who do not possess superior intelligence.

Quickly he removes his street clothes to reveal a tightly wound body. He is 6-0, 190 pounds, not large by baseball standards, but his torso tapers from the wide, sloping shoulder of a light-heavyweight to a narrow, rippled waist and the hips of a sprinter.

If he is not unduly quiet—he frequently rags teammates but somehow seems to retain a serious demeanor—neither does he display the raucousness that is as much a part of the pre-game clubhouse scene as are towels and the odor of liniment.

He has studied, analyzed, improvised a game that represents much of his life, and in the minutes before he goes forth to ply his trade, he is sober.

"I hate like hell to lose, but I suppose nobody knows it. I try to be as relaxed as I can. I suppose I'm as tense as anybody else inside."

Aaron exudes a confidence which has, of course, been borne of success repeated so often as to have become routine. "To be frank, I've always been able to do what I said I would do."

In the clubhouse, the Braves—who affectionately call him "Supe" for superstar—defer to him in the small ways that indicate he is chief of the tribe. He is older than any of them; works as hard or harder than any of them. So no one in the room is respected as he is. "His biggest ability is to ignite a team," says one baseball man.

And in his own mind, Aaron fights the aging process, knows that a rubber band does not lose its effectiveness any faster than a professional athlete. "Somewhere in the back of your mind you know that one bad year, or even a bad month or a bad week, will have everyone speculating about your crumbling abilities. So you do put out extra, not only for their sake but for your own. You just hate not to do justice to a talent you have taken pride in and dedicated yourself to your whole life."

Certainly any portrait of Henry Aaron the ballplayer must begin with Henry Aaron the hitter. He is extraordinarily well named, for the biblical priest Aaron is best known for carrying a big stick, albeit one that sprouted almonds.

Henry Aaron's bat sprouts home runs, and it is easily sensed as he walks to home plate that he is, despite his relatively modest stature, a power hitter. Overdeveloped thighs give him sort of a swaggering duckwaddle and he moves toward the plate purposefully, directly. Once in the batter's box, he rarely leaves it, squaring himself at right angles and then twisting his body slightly toward the catcher. A master of the art of one-upmanship at the plate, Aaron slowly and methodically goes through a ritual before acknowledging the pitcher. Placing the butt of the bat on the ground and leaning the knob against a thigh, he looks straight ahead as he calmly places the batting helmet upon his head, adjusting it with both hands. Suddenly he turns cold eyes over his left shoulder at the pitcher, and lifts the bat high, cocking it and waving it in tight, vicious circles; a man coiled like a snake.

The bat, made by Hillerich & Bradsby Co. in a huge, drab building at Finzer and Jacob Streets in Louisville, is, ironically, a slimmed-down version of the ones used by Ruth, although 11 ounces lighter and a half-inch shorter than the gargantuan 44-ouncers wielded by the man whose shadow he eclipsed. In fact, early in his career, Aaron used the Babe Ruth model bat exclusively.

But the bat does not hold the secret of Aaron's power, for it is vested in wrists two inches larger than Muhammed Ali's. Amid all the speculation over Aaron's physical tools, his wrists were often overlooked. "He just sees something white and hits it with a stick," wrote New York baseball writer Tommy Holmes, placing Aaron's natural reflexes in company with the beauty of Mickey Vernon's perfectly level swing and Ted Williams' eyesight and Stan Musial's concentration.

But Rogers Hornsby scoffed at such learned observations. "He's a wrist hitter . . . all the good hitters are. That's where they get their power, snapping into the ball. Somebody said he has marvelous hips, only you don't hit the ball with your hips. What he has is a smooth pivot that gives him power, lets him get his weight behind the ball."

And some baseball men were not interested in delving into the reasons Hank Aaron hit a baseball so hard, content merely with the results. "You'd have to be crazy to tell him anything about hitting," former Brave manager Fred Haney observed.

Any inquiry into Aaron's skills with the bat would, of course, have a natural starting place with those who play straight man for him, the pitchers.

None has been so widely quoted on the subject of Henry Aaron, hitter, as former St. Louis lefthander Curt Simmons, the pitcher Aaron acknowledges his toughest foe ever.

Simmons is reputed to have observed, "Sneaking a fastball past Henry is like trying to sneak the sun past a rooster." Simmons isn't so sure he ever made the statement, but it has been attributed to him and he likes the line so he says, "Go ahead and say I said it."

Other pitchers have also resorted to levity in discussing Aaron. Asked how he pitched to the Brave star, the Mets' Tug McGraw told an interviewer, "the same as anybody else, except don't let the ball go." Steve Blass of the Pirates, in Atlanta to take part in a bowling tournament Aaron runs for charity, said, "It seems like I'm always coming to Atlanta to do a benefit for Henry. Most of the time, though, it's held at the ballpark. Soon as I come on the field I start looking around for him . . . hoping I don't see him."

Aaron's biggest fan among the current pitchers is the Mets' Tom Seaver, who says Aaron was his "boyhood hero. He was always first with me. I thought of Aaron as excellence. He was so much fun to sit and watch because he was consistent, dedicated, and yet capable of making the game look so easy to play."

Aaron's dedication—not to mention his skill in reading pitchers—was confirmed for Seaver 10 years later when he reached the major leagues. The first time he faced Aaron, Seaver's third pitch was an inside fastball and Aaron grounded into a doubleplay. "I was a rookie, but I was trying to learn," Seaver said. "The next time Aaron came up, I thought *inside fastball-doubleplay*. He hit an inside fastball four-hundred feet for a home run. I learned something else. Pitchers weren't the only ones who could think: Henry Aaron had been thinking too. *Kid pitcher. Got me to hit into a doubleplay last time on an inside fastball. Bet he'll come with it again.* Our love affair ended there."

Explains Houston's Claude Osteen, who has given up 13 of Aaron's home runs to top the list of active pitchers, "He's got that great instinct. He knows what's coming. You might cross him once in a while, but not often."

One player, Baltimore outfielder Paul Blair, attributes Aaron's skill to a lack of the fear, which, to some degree, affects all hitters. "Don Drysdale always tried to hit Aaron in the ass," Blair said. "Not every once in awhile . . . every time. But no matter how many times he did it, the first time he threw the ball over the plate, Aaron would hit a line drive."

And what does the subject himself say of his craft? "Guessing what the pitcher is going to throw is eighty per cent of hitting. The other twenty per cent is just execution. All good hitters guess a lot; you're a dumb hitter if you don't guess some."

Aaron typically does not indulge in over-think about hitting. Some things time has taught him are mandatory. Guessing. Staying in good physical condition. "I'm not a teetotaler, I'll take an occasional drink. And I do smoke. But I take care of myself. Anything that interferes with my hitting, I don't do. And I keep a mental book on what pitchers throw me. When I'm hitting well, I can tell what a pitch will be when it's about halfway to the plate. I suppose it's the brain up there ticking."

The brain ticks when Aaron is in the field, too. In a game two years ago, decoying a Cincinnati runner by making him think he was going to make a catch, Aaron drew the praise of the Reds' Pete Rose. "The guy held up thinking Henry was going to make the catch, and he only moved up one base instead of two," Rose said. "Because of that, he don't score on a hit and we don't get a run and we lose. Aaron beat us without getting a hit that day. That's the sign of a real pro. Don't let anyone tell you he doesn't hustle. He plays as hard as anyone."

In the outfield, Aaron often ignores fly balls that twist foul into the stands. "I know when the ball's going into the stands," he says. "What would it prove to run over there. That's false hustle. I hustle when I have to."

Former Brave manager Bobby Bragan has always

ranked Aaron one of the game's fine defensive outfielders. "If you need a shoestring catch, he'll make it. He does whatever is needed. Like Joe DiMaggio did it."

Aaron presents a similar picture on the bases. He has reduced stealing to a personal art, although age has caused him to rarely attempt to run the past several years. But once during his career he stole 24 times in 24 attempts; stole 31 bases in 1963, and a teammate said, "He could have stolen a hundred if he'd had to."

"I'm no Maury Wills, but I know when to run and I've had some success stealing," said Aaron. "I'm convinced most pitchers make up their minds before they step up to the rubber if they'll try a pickoff. Never mind how I know. It's been very useful."

So is the durability which kept Aaron in the chase of Ruth's record. He has had few injuries in his career, a fact his doctor, Robert E. Wells, attributed in some part to Aaron's low-key personality.

"He not only gives the external appearance of being a placid man, but he doesn't have the physical symptoms that go with emotional disturbances," Dr. Wells said after the 1971 season had ended. "He has the body of a man six or eight years younger. As far as his physical condition goes, there's no reason he should quit playing baseball. Speaking from a medical standpoint, I am confident Hank will pass Babe Ruth's record."

Going into the 1972 season, Aaron would need 76 home runs to erase, at least statistically, Ruth's standard. He would, he had decided during the off-season, play two more years. But he "would quit" short of the mark if "I need fifteen or twenty to break it."

"There's no place in this game for forty-year-old players, and that's what I'll be in two more years. And as for playing at forty . . . well, you have to be kidding.

"I don't want to be playing just to go for a record."

He wouldn't.

12

Topping Willie

His knee ached. They'd drain the damn thing, and it would balloon again and they'd drain it again. And nobody had to tell him. His arm was shot. And Richards was telling people he'd like to trade him while the market was still hot. And Eddie was talking about him playing first base. And the team had gone sour because too many guys would rather play gin in the clubhouse than take extra batting practice. And they kept talking about pressure until he'd gotten to thinking about it. And he was 38. 38. Too old. Too tired to play day games after night games. Too old to play the second game of doubleheaders. Too old, period.

And, on top of and overshadowing everything else, there was Ruth. *You gonna' do it, Hank? You going to break the Babe's record? You getting uptight, Hank? You ever think about Maris? Does Mays have a shot, Hank? You better not break that record, Nigger.*

"Babe. Babe. Babe. Babe. Babe Ruth," Aaron sighed one night early in the 1972 season. The ghost had come to ride his back until the pursuit would end, and only now had Aaron come to appreciate what the next two years were to be like.

In February, he had become the highest paid baseball player in history, extracting a three-year, $600,000 contract from the Braves that was geared to the pursuit of Ruth's record and the end of Aaron's career as a player.

Standing between Aaron and Ruth were several obstacles, the major one a creaky right knee injured late in the 1971 season. The Braves wanted him to have surgery; Aaron refused. "If I were younger, an operation would be the thing to do. But at my age, I don't think I should take the chance."

So the year began with Aaron hobbling about. The lethargy which had been the identifying characteristic of the Braves held sway in 1972, so much so that they seemed to exist as nothing more than a backdrop for the Ruth vs. Aaron passion play.

But, for the first time, the team seemed capable of dragging Hank Aaron down to its level. Never was Atlanta in the race for the N.L. Western division pennant. Luman Harris was fired with 50 games left and replaced by Eddie Mathews, whose vigorous attempts to shake up a lazy ball club also failed.

Harris and Mathews faced several serious problems, the biggest of which was the lack of a first baseman. Orlando Cepeda's ravaged knees had forced his trade to Oakland for another fallen idol, Denny McLain, and when Harris desperately needed someone to fill the breach, Aaron was the man. He had played 71 games at first during the 1971 season and made only three errors, but in 1972 it was painfully obvious he was not a first baseman. Only one other first baseman in the league— the Pirates' Willie Stargell—was making more errors. Aaron's poor fielding affected his hitting. And general manager Paul Richards, about to be fired and desperate because of it, told acquaintances it just might be time to get rid of Aaron.

"He looks like he's over the hill," Richards said. "He can't play first base. He's a miserable first baseman. He can't play right field; his arm's gone. He's not hitting. He's making two hundred thousaand dollars a year. The gate attraction he is, I ought to be able to make a hell of a deal for him right now."

Undoubtedly Atlanta's *in absentia* president, Bill Bartholomay, squelched such talk and it died completely in June when Richards left the club. But it was indicative of the straits in which Hank Aaron discovered himself in 1972.

The first base experiment was compassionately ended by Mathews. "It wasn't difficult . . . I only told Hank I wanted to save his life," Mathews said of Aaron's return to right field.

But the solution was not complete. Aaron could no longer make the long throws from right. "The ball was leaving my hand as fast," he said, "but it was traveling slower and dying sooner. Base runners were taking advantage of me. I was hurting the club."

The answer was a permanent move to left field, and Aaron accepted it graciously, as he did the undeniable fact he was growing old. But he viewed the aging process optimistically. "I have an appreciation for things in life that I wasn't capable of appreciating before. I'm not afraid to speak out, and I was before."

In toto, the 1972 season was a disaster for both Atlanta and Aaron. The Braves never challenged, were in fact the only team in the West to never own or share the lead. They finished fourth, 25 games behind pennant-winning Cincinnati.

Hank Aaron did not fare much better. His average (.265) was a career low; his RBIs (77) the fewest he had managed since his rookie year. But he did hit 34 home runs to creep within 41 of Ruth and he did cause considerable revision of the record book. On June 10, Aaron hit career homer No. 649 to edge ahead of Willie Mays in the race for Ruth's crown. RBI No. 1,199 on June 28th shoved him ahead of Lou Gehrig for second place on the all-time list. His 660th home run, which came in August, set a record as the most ever hit by a player with one team.

And they still held him in abiding affection in Atlanta, where the stands were constantly festooned with banners reading: "We love Henry," and "715 Comes Next" and "Hammerin' Hank Is Our Hero."

On July 25th, he repaid their affection. In the sixth inning of a soporific All-Star Game, he hit a Gaylord Perry pitch so hard the saliva came off it. When the ball disappeared into the left-center bullpen there came from the stands an ungodly roar that threatened for long, long moments to never end.

An outpouring of love and gratitude, it set Aaron's nerve ends to twanging. The crowd stood and beat its hands together so hard and so long that the Mets' Tug McGraw said he could "feel the vibrations in the bullpen." Later, Aaron, whose all-star career had been modest at best, couldn't quite believe it.

"I think that was the most emotional home run I've ever hit in my life," he said. "Nothing like it ever happened to me before. It's impossible to describe the thrill."

But there were few such thrills for Aaron in 1972. He was fighting the battle no man can ever win; against the years. "I get tired," he said. "I got tired last year. It's not so much playing, it's the travel. Going to the West Coast, sleeping and eating habits change and it's hard to be ready to play baseball. The reflexes change, too. They can't come back as quick at my age. I know I have trouble with pitchers on the coast and when we come back to Atlanta, I hit them all right."

166

In 1972, Aaron had trouble with the pitchers everywhere. For years he had thought that no single activity in sport was quite so difficult or tiring as "taking a round bat and using it to hit a round ball, squarely."

"As much as I respect other sports, it takes a special talent to go out there and hit the ball every day. It's tougher now than ever. The pitching is so much better. When I first came up only two clubs, us and Brooklyn, had real good, deep pitching staffs. Now every club has depth. A starter goes five, six innings, then they bring in a fresh one. A hitter has no relief."

And when there was not weariness, there was Aaron's right knee. It was drained seven times in 1972 and shortly after the All-Star Game, he began wearing a brace on it. "Willie McCovey said it helped him and since his knee is a lot worse than mine, I thought I'd try it. It's helped a lot."

Overriding everything else was *The Record*. Suddenly in midsummer, the American public seemed to become aware that the grandest of all sports records was under serious attack. Aaron could go nowhere, engage in no activity, without first appraising his chances to surpass Ruth.

His answers were varied, but because he is an immensely polite man, no questioner was turned away. "I'd say I have a better than even chance of doing it," he said throughout the season. "It means a lot to me to be as close to the record as I am. I'm not concerned about it. In fact, I try not to think about it except when somebody brings it up."

And somebody was forever bringing it up, as they would until he had dispatched Ruth onto another page of the record book. Finally, and understandably, Aaron developed stock answers to the stock questions, which dropped upon him as though they were some form of a Chinese water torture.

"I have supreme confidence. I feel there is nothing on the field that I cannot do. I've always felt that way. Sometimes it doesn't work out, but I feel I can do it.

"When I think of my chances of breaking the record, I can't emphasize the man batting behind me enough. Ruth had one of the greatest players to ever play the game behind him (Lou Gehrig). I've been fortunate, too. There were Eddie Mathews and Joe Adcock and Wes Covington, and then when they began fading away, there came Joe Torre and Rico Carty and Early Williams.

"I feel fine. Barring injuries, I see no reason why I shouldn't. . . ."

But the man of whom Houston pitcher Claude Osteen once said "slapping a rattlesnake across the face with back of your hand it safer than trying to fool him," did not always hide his feelings behind platitudes.

"To be frank, it is not as important to me as it is to baseball," he finally said of his pursuit of Ruth. "The only thing I ever thought about was to be as good as I could. I never thought about being the greatest ballplayer or anything . . . just to be as good as I could."

In time, Aaron came to stoically endure the endless conversation his quest seemed to inspire, becoming snappish only occasionally, as he was when he learned one National League manager was making bets he would not break the record. "I know who he is and I ought to put the commissioner on him."

But mostly he accepted the pressure easily. "At first, all the talk bugged me," he told Dave Anderson of *The New York Times* in August. "But now it's like waking up and having breakfast. It's part of my day. People are always wishing me luck, but I don't know if all of them really mean it. My mail is sixty to forty for me to stay healthy and break it, but some people think that because he had three thousand fewer at-bats than I will, that I wouldn't really be breaking his record."

"But when people ask me if I want to break his record, I'd be telling a lie if I said no. Pressure? I don't really know what it is. I've been playing this game too long to all of a sudden think I've got to play under pressure the next two years. I don't think the pressure's going to be that much trouble. I've always been able to handle a situation."

There were, however, moments in 1972 when Aaron had to shake himself to be certain he wasn't dreaming; that a poor black kid out of Toulminville was really breathing on the neck of a legend.

"You know, it's hard for me to believe that I might have a shot at Ruth's record," he said one day. "It's just one of those things you never even think about until one day you suddenly realize that here is something great that might be within your reach. Why, when I broke into baseball I wasn't even a home run hitter. I weighed one hundred sixty pounds and I hit a total of nine at Eau Claire, Wisconsin. It wasn't much to get excited over."

Others were excited over Aaron's attack on the record. "All black players in the major leagues identify with Hank Aaron," said Ernie Banks, the grand old man of the Chicago Cubs. "Not only because he's going for a tremendous record . . . but because he's a tremendous man."

One black man in the major leagues in particular identified with Hank Aaron. His name was Willie Mays, and in 1972 while Aaron was poking his hand into the stars, Mays was frantically treading water in a bid not to bring dishonor to his brilliant achievement.

By 1972 it had become apparent that it would be Aaron, and not Mays, who would challenge Ruth. In temperament, Mays was much like the last man to reach for Ruthian heights, Roger Maris.

In 1961, Maris had hit 61 home runs, paying a stiff

price in nerve ends in the process. In September of that year, Maris would after each game, homer or not, hold a press conference in the New York Yankee clubhouse. Removing a sopping shirt, he would prop himself in his wide locker and a clubhouse man would hand him a can of beer. Whereupon Maris—called "Roger the Red Ass" by more than one acquaintance—would do battle with the press. His abrasive manner came to irritate almost everyone with whom he had contact and before Maris eclipsed Ruth's season record of 60 home runs, he had been roundly booed in every American League city, accused of being a malingerer, and been able to count those who called him friend with the fingers on one hand. "The games were the easy part," he said later of the immense pressure. "Those hours were the only times when I got any relief from the pressure."

Mays, too, became more abrasive than ever in 1972 when it became clear Aaron had outstripped him in the two-man race for Ruth's record. He had come into 1972 needing 87 home runs to top Ruth. But he was faced with handicaps which were insurmountable. He was 39 and the years suddenly were weighing heavily upon him, his batting stroke slowed now so that during the season he had asked a group of reporters, with tears in his eyes, "Do I really look that bad?" And there were vicious left-to-right winds that blew across expansive Candlestick Park and wreaked havoc on long-ball hitters. Before year's end, Jimmy (The Greek) Snyder laid odds of 4-to-1 against Mays breaking Ruth's record and even Mays seemed to be in agreement when he began talking of what might have been rather than what was going to be.

"I was in the Army two years and I was young and strong at that time," he said. "I should have added fifty, maybe sixty home runs to my total in those years. But

Laughing it up with Flip Wilson at filming of "The Flip Wilson Show" in Hollywood.

A guy named Roger—Maris, 61 homers one year—says hello to a guy named Hank in Atlanta.

now I don't believe in goals. I just keep playing as long as I can help the club."

Later the Giants would shunt him to the New York Mets to be rid of his contract and there is evidence Mays was a long time in loosening his grip on a dream. "Two years ago I didn't think I had a chance, but when you get so close, you think about playing a few more years."

Mays, who hit only eight home runs in 1972, gave ground to Aaron grudgingly. Asked if he thought Aaron would catch Ruth, Mays snapped: "He's got to catch me first." Later, Aaron smiled at the remark. "All that did when Willie said 'he's got to catch me first' was to give me some added incentive. I was in no fight with Willie. I wasn't after anyone's record. All I wanted was to do the best I could for Aaron. After he said that, though, I was consciously trying a little harder."

There is evidence, despite the protest of both to the contrary, that there was friction between Aaron and Mays. It was felt by many that Aaron was unhappy when Mays failed to appear on a television show with him during the 1972 season. Aaron, as might have been expected, denied it.

"I like to think that Willie and I have always been good friends," he said. "Contrary to what some people think, this never was a duel between me and Willie. We have respect for each other as friendly rivals. Obviously, I made catching him one of my goals, but whenever you set your sights, you reach for the top. And Willie has been the top."

Nevertheless, putting Mays in the shadows obviously pleased Aaron. "I've always read Mickey Mantle, Willie Mays . . . then Hank Aaron," he said. "I've worked awfully hard to get my name in front. I wasn't worried about catching Willie. I'm more concerned about catching Stan Musial in the front office."

Late in the 1972 season, after hundreds of nibbles at the edges of an answer to the question, Aaron finally put the meaning of the quest in personal perspective.

"When you're close to forty, you're at an age where the game becomes dull," he admitted. "You're thinking about quitting. But since the record is so close, I'd be denying myself the privilege if I didn't go for it. If I wasn't as close as I was, this would be my last year. But next year will definitely be my last one."

Next year. In 1973 Aaron felt Ruth's record would come tumbling down.

It almost did.

Not all the letter writers were pen pals, Hank and his secretary, Carla Koplin, discovered.

13

Living with a Ghost

It was a memorable spring.

In Korea, a bone-tired army was preparing to leave the country after seven agonizing years of combat. In Egypt, a young Army colonel was sweeping to power on the strength of promises to hurl the Israelites to the sea. In the U. S. Supreme Court, whites and blacks fought their quiet, unyielding war for or against social change. And the afternoon soap operas were repeatedly being pushed off national television so that the nation might study the anguish of an immensely powerful politician under extreme duress.

It was, of course, 1954.

That spring, Henry Louis Aaron hit his first major-league home run. In the time that has elapsed since that day: the French and American armies have bled deeply into the soil of Viet Nam and then left; Gamal Abdel Nasser rose to power, gloried in it. died and was replaced; the Supreme Court has sorted out a thousand racial disputes; Senator Joe McCarthy's abuses of power were drawn to the bar of justice and dispatched, replaced later by those of Richard Nixon, and three major figures in American history rose to power, used it, and were assassinated.

The world has turned; wars have been fought and settled; peace has glimmered seductively a half-dozen times; grass has made the transition from something to be mowed to something to be smoked; hemlines have risen, fallen, disappeared; change has become mankind's modus operandi. Newness abounds—the New Morality, the New Religion the New Sex, and so on.

And Henry Louis Aaron long endures, so that in the spring of 1973, pretty much what he has always been, he stood ready to bring one more bit of newness to the world; to return to the dust one more relic of the past.

He would—"if I don't get hit by a truck"—render George Herman Ruth merely one more of the many fallen idols. In the process, Aaron would become something of a villian and experience the personal pressure known only to those who linger in the national spotlight. He was killing off a legend, and there is a price to be paid for such destruction, as Rocky Marciano discovered by turning Joe Louis into a hulking wreck. "I hated to do it," Marciano had said. Replied Louis, "Tell Rocky not to feel so bad. He was only doing his job."

And that, precisely, was the mood Hank Aaron adopted in the spring of 1973 as he readied himself to answer the year's, perhaps the millenium's, greatest sports question: Would Hank Aaron be the man who beat the Babe?

"It's the biggest challenge of my life; this is going to be my most interesting year in baseball," Aaron said at West Palm Beach in March. At that time, he sought to make several things perfectly clear. It would not be unrealistic, he observed, to think he would break Ruth's record in 1973. If that were the case, he would retire at the season's end. Further, if he did not break the record, he did not believe anyone else ever would. His attempt would suffer because pitchers would try to pitch around him or walk him, but would be enhanced by winter trades that had brought some good, young hitters to the Braves. Certainly, he understood the pressure would grow so enormous that he would come to hate the very sound of the word. He also noted that, at 39, he was appreciative of such small favors as the Dodgers, Cardinals and Padres moving their fences in to help their own hitters.

"Sometimes I can get through a whole day without thinking about Ruth," he laughed. "The other day I was having a nice time playing golf with a friend when some guy ran over and asked if I thought I could break Ruth's record. I said to myself, 'Oh, no.' That would happen a lot last year and it got so after games I would just go back to my hotel room. It can be lonely."

For company, Aaron had the ghost of Ruth, but Braves' manager Eddie Mathews wasn't worried. "He'll handle this," Mathews said. "He's the same man, one day to the next. And another thing. He's had time to prepare mentally. This has been building up over several seasons. What happened to Roger Maris won't happen to Henry Aaron."

At the outset, Aaron set two goals for 1973: 35 home runs and a resolution not to let the chase of Ruth hurt the ballclub. "I'll just go up and try to help the club, play the game the same way I've always played it. Some people may think I'm selfish if I go for the home run, but I will if the situation calls for it. Why change after 19 years? I just want to hit the ball hard."

So when the season began, it was 42 and counting. "After all these years, I'm going to find out if I can do the job," Aaron mused. "I'll just do the best I can with everything, including the pressure and attention. I can't go into a shell and hide.

When in the early days of the season the questions began in earnest, Aaron's answers to them were unchanging. "Somebody can come along and hit eight hundred home runs and it's never going to mean as much as Babe Ruth's record," he said softly. "They're always going to talk about him and his seven-fourteen. No matter who comes along and hits more than he did, people are just not going to accept the fact that somebody's capable of breaking that record. So I've got to play baseball the way I know I can play it, and relax, and do things the best I can."

Hank Aaron was right. There were those who would not accept his attack on Ruth's immortality. And before the season was a month old, and while he was struggling in the throes of a slump, the hate mail began to pour in. *Who are you to think you can break Ruth's record, Nigger? You black nigger bastard. Go back to Africa where you belong, you black son of a bitch.*

Aware he would receive a flood of mail, although unaware of its nature, the Braves had provided Aaron with a secretary, Carla Koplin, and a small office at the stadium. The young secretary tried to shield Aaron, but he was adamant. He had always answered his mail personally, and "I want to read what they're saying." What he read made him sick at heart and angry.

"You have to be black in America to know how sick some people are," he said. "My mail is about 75-25 against me. Most of it is racial. They call me 'nigger' and every other bad word you can imagine.

"If I was white, all America would be proud of me."

Some of the letters, many of them questioning Aaron's masculinity and the legitimacy of his children, reached his wife's home. They horrified the Braves. "You have to be concerned," said Atlanta executive Donald Davidson.

"There are a lot of crazy people around. We've proved that in this country."

Undoubtedly, Aaron's activities in behalf of blacks inspired some of the hate mail. He had donated $5,500 to a fund for sickle cell anemia research and ran a celebrity bowling tournament for black charities the previous year. He was also honorary chairman of the Atlanta NAACP chapter.

His reaction to the hate mail was typical. "The more they push me, the more I want the record. Some people seem to sense that I'm getting into an area where no black man has a right to be. But I can't do anything about the mail."

But he did. He made a simple statement with a smile. "What do they want me to do—stop hitting home runs?" he said. "I have no intention of making people forget Babe Ruth. I just want to be sure they remember Hank Aaron."

His words struck a chord. In weeks the tide had turned. "The mail is almost all favorable now," Carla Koplin reported. "I think the silent majority is being heard from."

Certainly some sort of majority was. Requests poured into Carla Koplin for hanks of Aaron's hair, dirt from around home plate at Atlanta Stadium, pictures, autographs, personal appearances by Aaron and invitations for him to visit vacation sites. Frank Sinatra and, yes, Alabama's George Wallace were among many of the well-known people who sent telegrams of encouragement and Atlanta mayor Sam Massell wrote ". . . You are Atlanta's hero . . . don't let the bums get you down . . . when we tell our grandchildren we saw you hit the big one, we want to know *you* knew at the time that we were your friends."

The kids, as might be expected, wrote the best stuff. "I hope you catch up with Baby Root . . . We love you,

Hanko-Po ... I had a pet gopher snake named Henry; it was the nicest snake I ever had ... I got your picture and autograph December 29th and it was my best Christmas present ... I remember you when I bite into an Oh Henry candy bar; I hope you break the other guy's record ... If I could meet you, I would be so happy I would walk upside down."

One night when the Braves were in Houston, Astros brass had a message flashed on the Dome's huge scoreboard: "Mr. Aaron. For every one of those bad letters you receive, there are thousands pulling for you. Good luck in your homer quest ... after you leave the Astrodome."

In time some 30,000 letters would flow through Carla Koplin's hands, most of them encouraging Aaron, who in time became more candid about his run at Ruth.

"Ruth's record is about the last thing in professional sports that whites can hang on to—the legendary record of the Sultan of Swat. But I can't think about that. If I'm a target, I can only worry about my job, and doing it good. I think it's good for America. The world keeps going on. Kids today can relate to me. And besides, why should they relate to a ballplayer who quit playing thirty-five years ago?

"I think it also gives black kids hope. It shows them that anything is possible today. Maybe they can't be a ballplayer like me, but they can strive for excellence and be a good doctor or lawyer or anything. I believe I would have tried to be the best at whatever I did, even if it was being a dirt-shoveler."

The pro-Aaron letters reached a threshold the day he received one signed by a thousand Minneapolis schoolchildren. But to be pro-Ruth was not necessary to be anti-Aaron.

Babe Ruth had been a part of the youth of more than one generation and those who bewailed the loss of many artifacts of the past, suffered to think that even the mighty Babe would fall. A spokesman for the group was Washington *Post* columnist Chalmers M. Roberts.

"It is," wrote Roberts, "simply a matter of moorings. The Empire State Building may not be the world's tallest any more, but it is for me . . . Most of us are captives of our memories. And that goes for me and George Herman Ruth, the Babe." Roberts summed up his thoughts with the observation that he wished Aaron luck, but were he successful, Aaron would "have knocked a great big hole in my nostalgia."

If Aaron did not fully compreheend the emotions he was stirring before the season began, he was soon to understand their intensity. Although his average hovered in the low .200 range in the first month of the year, Aaron was hitting the ball hard, so hard that 10 of his first 20 hits were home runs. Perhaps it seemed to some Atlanta fans he had forsaken the team for the quest. In any case, the first week in May an ugly incident occurred at Atlanta Stadium.

A clot of males seated within hearing of Aaron began assailing him, one fan particularly obnoxious. "Hey, Nigger, you're no Ruth . . . how come a nigger son of a bitch like you makes so much money and strikes out so much. . . ."

Aaron took it for eight innings. In the ninth, he strode to the stands, waved a clenched fist and hollered. "I'm coming up there and kick in your butt if you don't shut your rotten mouth." The man shouted back but was pulled into his seat by his wife and later removed from the stadium.

"I tried to ignore him as long as I could," Aaron said. "Something snapped. If I strike out and someone hollers I'm a bum, that's part of it. But those guys were personal, vicious and obscene, and I'd had all I was going to take."

In fact, Aaron had been taking it in Atlanta for a long time. "It's been going on for two years, that racial stuff. I don't have to take that crap from some loud-mouthed redneck. His wife probably slaps him at home, and he sticks a big cigar in his mouth and doesn't say a word, then comes down here and takes it out on me. It's the kind of aggravation I don't have to take. I hope the club can help me.

The club did, especially moved by Aaron's remark to New York *Daily News* columnist Dick Young that "I'd love to play someplace else, to be frank. It's worse because it's happening in my own ballpark, in front of people I've played for in hundreds of games. I try to pass it off as ignorance. I know it happens all over the world, but I'm concerned about Atlanta."

There was great irony in whites baiting Aaron because he was bearing down on a record established by Ruth, who because of the cast of his features and vague background had been called "Nigger" by bench-jockeys throughout his career. An acutely insensitive man, Ruth was particularly sensitive about that single epithet, once breaking into an opposing team's clubhouse after a World Series game to challenge New York Giant utilityman Johnny Rawlings. "If you ever call me that again . . . ," Ruth was saying when he noticed reporters taking notes. "Please, fellas, don't write anything about this," said the retreating Ruth, who paused at the door to add, "I'm sorry this happened. I don't mind being called a son of a bitch or a bastard, but lay off that personal stuff."

As the 1973 season wore on, the Braves settling into their comfortable niche in the lower depths of the National League West, the pressure continued to mount for Aaron, still struggling to elevate his average although he had hit 19 home runs at the All-Star Game break in June.

Ironically, throughout a brilliant 19-year career Aaron had hungered for national attention, and now performing in the world's largest fishbowl was working hardships upon him. The number of autograph-seekers prowling the corridors of the Braves' road hotels increased to such a degree that traveling secretary Don Davidson began registering Aaron as "Victor Koplin," the last name in honor of Aaron's secretary, the first a product of Davidson's imagination. "Pretty soon I'm going to register him as Babe Ruth," laughed the diminutive Davidson, who, told in Houston there was a rumor Aaron had been shot, retorted "if Henry had been shot, I'm sure he would've called and told me."

But the shock of the hate mail had unnerved Brave officials and they hired a special bodyguard for Aaron and requested the league provide two special policemen to escort Aaron to and from the Brave bus in each National League city. And after a black fan was shot at a game in Pittsburgh, 20 policemen were assigned as Aaron's security guard there. Also, there were no end of people who just had to have a few minutes of Aaron's time. One night there were two state governors to see him in the Atlanta clubhouse and on another occasion a group of Japanese newsmen besieged him. "Only one of them spoke English," reported Brave public relations director Bob Hope, "and he only knew seven words. Two of them were 'Hank Aaron.'"

Aaron stoically continued to deny the pressure was getting to him. "I'm not Roger Maris; I can handle you guys," he would laugh with reporters. But a friend said, "He's only human, so he's got to be feeling it and he might be better off if he showed it instead of bottling it up." And Estella Aaron said of her seemingly placid son, "All this fuss. Oh, it boils him so. He says he don't ever have a moment alone." It rankled Aaron when he was asked one night if he was taking tranquilizers—"No!"—but on doctor's orders he drank a glass of sherry at breakfast to quiet a nervous stomach.

"I'm as excited as I can get," he said, "but I can't go out and click my heels. That's just the way I am. The reason I may not be emotional about all of this is because I've been doing it for nineteen years."

But, for perhaps the millionth time, a newsman asked about the pressure. "There isn't any," Aaron insisted. Asked what he would write if he were covering Aaron, Hank laughed, "I wouldn't be here, I'd be over covering the Eastern division race because it's more exciting."

Only when the subject of his right to challenge Ruth arose, did Aaron ever lose his usually unassailable cool. Bumper stickers reading "Aaron is Ruthless" riled him. "Why can't they understand I'm just trying to do my job?" he asked. "When the final curtain comes down my record will speak for itself. I don't have to take a back seat to any player, today, yesterday, or any day. They're not giving me anything."

Certainly the pitchers weren't. Those who walked him or struck him out were booed in their own ballparks. Complained the Dodgers' Claude Osteen, "If you fall behind him two on nothing or three on one, your own fans boo." But pitchers became increasingly wary of Aaron and it was the Dodgers who walked him five straight times one night. In his first 40 games, Aaron was walked 28 times. "I think the pitchers are concentrating more every time I get up to the plate," Aaron said. "It's going to be a lot harder for me to break the record than people think."

The fact that the Braves hitting before Aaron (Ralph Garr) and after him (Dusty Baker) were not exactly tearing the cover from the ball didn't help. But it was age ("the balls you used to hit out of the park you foul off now") and cautious pitching ("I'm not getting much to hit but the pitch I can hit, I can hit out of the park") that affected Aaron the most during the 1973 season. And, of course, the ghost of Ruth.

"I didn't hear Babe's name once," Aaron said during an off-day in July, "until I turned on the television. I started watching a dull football game, so I switched channels. I got a roundtable discussion program and, sure enough, they started talking about Babe Ruth and Hank Aaron."

In late July, they were talking about Ruth and Aaron in Las Vegas, too. Jimmy the Greek made it 3-to-1 against Aaron breaking the record before the season ended; 2-to-1 against tying it, and 14-to-1 against a homer each time Aaron came to the plate.

On July 20th, Aaron hit No. 699 off young Philadelphia righthander Wayne Twitchell and it had come to crunch. Suddenly, the entire country seemed to stop what it was doing and turn its eyes on Atlanta. Before it had been the baseball fans watching Henry Aaron's assault on Ruthian heights; now everyone was caught up in what the Braves' front office rightfully billed as "the greatest sports story in history."

Certainly it was nothing less. And the gut drama of it was just now building.

Robert Winborne, 18, retrieved Aaron's 700th homer and the exchange rate was 700 silver dollars.

14

Wait'll Next Year

No, the man insisted, he was not a nut. He was a base-ball fan, "a lover of sports." Jim Pry nodded. He was busy, the law firm of Myers, Spurlock, Sears and Pry being one of the busiest in Bucyrus, a manufacturing town of 13,000 located in north central Ohio in a crook of the Sandusky River. The client explained his request. He wanted the baseball Hank Aaron hit for home run No. 715. He would pay $10,000 for it. Pry explained the money would have to be placed in escrow to give his offer credibility. The man wrote out a check and placed it on deposit in a Bucyrus bank.

"This is a legitimate thing," Pry said. "If someone calls, I'm ready to hop on a plane and go get the ball."

The offer stood for two weeks. Another "lover of sport" topped it by $5,000.

America had the fever, and in the long, hot summer of 1973, it watched and waited for Hank Aaron to put Babe Ruth at least one step into the shade of baseball history.

If he had been virtually ignored throughout the years, now the nation had clasped him to its breast. The name Henry Aaron became etched in the country's frontal lobes. Here, we came to perceive, was a truly stupendous piece of history in the making. Or the unmaking. Here was a man scaling the frame of the grandest record in all of sport. Here, by God, was a continuing event a man could sink his teeth into and watch unfolding a bit at a time, the better to savor it.

Everyone suddenly wanted a piece of the action. None wanted it more avidly than the National Broadcasting Company, which announced rather pontifically, "It is altogether fitting that we give this event of national importance the coverage it warrants." This was a case of Baseball Commissioner Bowie Kuhn and the television moguls reacting to charges by the nation's sportswriters that the overtaking of Ruth was largely being ignored by both TV and the commissioner's office. NBC reported that when Aaron reached No. 710, it would have a crew on hand to tape each of his appearances at the plate and would interrupt network programming to show 714 and 715. Also, another NBC crew would shoot more than 30 miles of film for a documentary to be seen during telecasting of the 1973 World Series.

Not to be outdone by the electronic medium, *Time* magazine had a reporter following Aaron around for weeks for a cover story. *Newsweek* did likewise. *Ebony* hit the stands with a cover story in midsummer. Media people swirling around Aaron—in addition to the magazine writers there were reporters from 20 newspapers trailing him around most of the last half of the 1973 season—were dismayed to discover him colorless. A man free of the neuroses which make for interesting copy. A man downright normal.

But since his mission was unique, interest in him continued to heighten. Especially in Atlanta, where it must be noted he was most marketable. The lighted "Welcome to Atlanta" board at Hartsfield International Airport was converted into an Aaron countdown barometer. Three Atlanta-based companies, Coca Cola, Delta Airlines and Atlanta Life Insurance Co., chipped in a total of $11,000 for a Hank Aaron Scholarship Committee. The Atlanta Chamber of Commerce embarked on what it loftily described as "the most elaborate program of any city honoring a single sports individual in history." Both Atlanta newspapers were busy preparing Aaron supplements. The Braves announced they would contribute 700 silver dollars to the fan retrieving home run No. 700 and then give correspondiing amounts for each successive homer up through 715. To foil cheaters, they also announced each ball would be specially marked with invisible infra-red ink dots. The marquee on the Howard Johnson Motor Lodge near the stadium read, "See Hank Aaron Play. Just two blocks away." A billboard at the stadium carried Aaron's picture and the words ATLANTA SALUTES and then Aaron's signature. In the left corner in lights visible for miles was the number of the moment, changeable instantly when made necessary by another Aaron home run. As the lights caught the fans' eyes, the message coming through the loudspeaker was "everyone who witnesses the seven hundred fourteenth and seven hundred fifteenth home run will get a gold certificate ... you'll want to be here in person. They're mementoes you'll want to have of two historic events."

There were Aaron songs—"Move Over Babe, Here Comes Henry" and "Hammerin' Hank." And there were Aaron commercials. "On the field I let my bat do the talking; off the field I let my Brut do the talking," and "You shoulda' had your Wheaties, Hank." And there were dozens of Aaron contests, among the more exotic a two-week, all-expenses paid trip to Caesar's Palace in Las Vegas, which Red Smith referred to as "the American Lourdes." Business firms from such diversified cities as Cedar Rapids, Iowa, and Syracuse, New York, requested Aaron products. Women in halter tops, sporting baseball gloves and fishing nets, appeared in numbers in the left field seats of the nation's ballyards. Computer analysts, astrologists, and assorted clairvoyants rendered almost daily predictions on whether or not Aaron would pass Ruth in the summer of '73. A no less august body than the Wisconsin State Senate adopted a resolution expressing hope Aaron would break the record.

On every pitch, a time bomb ticked. "Are you enjoying this?" a reporter asked Aaron one night in late July. "I refuse to answer that," he grinned hugely, but no less an authority than veteran observer Dick Young of the New York *Daily News* wrote, "Underneath it all, I think he is eating it up. And he should."

"When he gets to seven hundred and twelve it's going to be like a countdown for a moon shot," said Brave traveling secretary Don Davidson. Agreeing, the Baseball Writers Association of America made arrangements for a special charter to carry sportswriters in pursuit of Aaron.

And then somebody noticed. Everyone was excited. Except Atlanta. The Braves, who had sold only 1,600 season tickets, weren't drawing flies by midsummer. Seldom were there 5,000 fans in the stadium; hardly ever did a crowd reach the 15,000 level of respectability considering what was occuring in the city during the 1973 season. There were various explanations, of course. The Braves had a lousy club (true). It was hot (not so true). Atlanta does not possess a baseball tradition (true). Blacks rarely attended in numbers (true). The city wasn't promoting the feat (false).

"Atlanta's a funny city," a black banker said. "We are more concerned with fine homes, fine automobiles and fine clothes. Nothing else matters."

A prominent black dentist had an explanation for the blacks' failure to turn out. "Today's black folk like super arrogant, flashy niggers. Aaron makes it look so easy, he's boring to watch."

"I thought it would all be overwhelming," said Donn Clendenon, an Atlanta resident and former major-league first baseman, "but it's not." The official response of the Chamber of Commerce was offered by Director of Community Relations Milt Lincoln, "Basically, I think everyone is kind of waiting, wondering 'Will he do it this year?'"

"One day, too late, the people here are going to realize what they had," a Brave official said bitterly, perhaps more pained by the lack of support for Aaron than any commercial consideration.

Montreal Expo general manager Jim Fanning had been wrong. "People will just want to take a look at him. They'll be coming out to see him take batting practice," Fanning had predicted. Not in Atlanta. A few seasons before Geraldine, the devilish creation of television comic Flip Wilson, had said, "Killer told me Hank Aaron was the mayor of Atlanta." But in the fading summer of 1973 it had become apparent Killer was badly mistaken.

Braves' season-ticket holder Jack Williams thought "it's a disgrace to baseball. It makes me sick to my stomach." But the pain Aaron felt must've been in his heart.

"I've got a job to do," he said when the lack of attendance began being publicized. "It doesn't make any difference to me if there are seven hundred and fifty people watching or seventy-five thousand." But they were just words; hardly the true feelings of a man who had spent years of sweat nearing a zenith only to discover his fans had been struck with a case of the yawns.

"I hate to attribute it all to race," he said later, "but I do think if it was Al Kaline or Ron Santo, it would be different. I think that's Atlanta for you, or the deep south."

Atlanta, a city that prides itself as an historical city, was largely ignoring history. But even Atlanta couldn't ignore July 21st.

Before a home game with the Phillies, Brave outfielder Dusty Baker watched Aaron field questions easily from a dozen reporters. "He's something else," Baker marveled. "I'll be more nervous shaking his hand after he gets the record than he will be breaking it."

It was true. As he promised, Aaron had handled the pressure of the news media; had not become another Roger Maris to later recall bitterly, "There were always people wanting something from me. It became personalities. I remember all the incidents. They're all still inside, but I don't talk about them. People got on my back."

People were not getting on Hank Aaron's back on the lovely evening of July 21st. The night before he had hit No. 699 off the Phils' Wayne Twitchell and on this night he would face a lefthander, Ken Brett. "Ain't Aaron beautiful?" asked Maris, who had been perhaps the most interested of all observers as Aaron pursued Ruth. "I'll be glad when it's over for him."

Before the game began, 18-year-old Robert Winborne of Atlanta settled comfortably into his seat in the left field stands and began reading *Point Counterpoint*, a weighty tome by Aldous Huxley. At five minutes before 6 o'clock, he put the book aside. As he did, Atlanta television personality Billye Williams dressed leisurely, thinking she had plenty of time to reach Atlanta Stadium before the game began. Mistakenly, she thought the starting time was 7 p.m., which she would later come to regret.

Before Billye Williams could reach the ballpark, her fiancee had become only the second player in history to hit his 700th home run. Aaron hit a low, inside fastball 400 feet, depositing Brett's pitch 10 rows into the lower left field stands, where Robert Winborne, whose dad had once played on the same baseball team with ex-New York Yankee star Snuffy Stirnweiss, outscrambled several fans for the ball.

"You can tell the commissioner he didn't groove it," Aaron grinned later, referring to statements made by several National League pitchers that they would be glad to make it easy for Aaron if he faced them needing only one home run to succeed Ruth. It was Aaron's 27th home run of the year and he felt he definitely could put an end to the pressure before the season concluded. "I think maybe I can do it this year," he said. "I feel that fourteen more this season isn't impossible.

"I'm glad it went into the seats so a kid like Robert could get the money. It's nice to get a nice, round figure. Now I can start counting down."

And the pressure? Aaron laughed. "When I get to seven-thirteeen, I suppose that's when I'll feel the pressure."

Telegrams flooded the Brave clubhouse after the 700th, but Aaron detected one missing. The one which should've come from the commissioner. "I was kind of disappointed that I didn't hear anything from him," Aaron said. "I didn't get one from President Nixon either . . . but I never expected one from him." Later, Bowie Kuhn would plead innocent to charges of ignoring Aaron: "He knows I'm one of his biggest rooters. I just wanted to wait to congratulate him face-to-face."

Home run No. 700, Aaron said, would not go to the Baseball Hall of Fame. In a rare show of emotion, he lashed out at the shrine's officials. "I sent them a lot of mementoes and they swept them under the rug," he said.

"It doesn't matter to me if any of my stuff goes there." Aaron's resentment went back three years. After sending Cooperstown his bats and balls from the 3,000th hit and 500th home run, he had been left out of a promotional booklet which the Hall of Fame distributed, although other active players such as Willie Mays were featured in it. The Cooperstown curators apologized, but forgot to include Aaron in the booklet the following year, as they had promised.

"I felt I had been slighted," Aaron explained. "I don't believe in holding grudges, though. It will all end here."

Aaron also held no grudge against Billye Williams. Two days before the 700th homer, it had been announced that Aaron and Mrs. Williams would be married in late autumn. The sloe-eyed, lovely Billye Williams, widow of a Morehouse College professor who had been active in the civil rights movement, conducts an early-morning television show, *Today in Atlanta*. She met Aaron on the show, although he had canceled two earlier scheduled appearances.

Mrs. Williams, who had taught English literature at Atlanta University prior to her husband's death, refused Aaron's first dinner invitation. "When I was a boy, that might've been enough to discourage me. But I was a man, so I asked her again. We both have been lonely and I thought we could spend some time together." Months later, Mrs. Williams sported a 2½-carat diamond engagement ring.

"I had never seen Henry play," Mrs. Williams said, in no way differentiating herself from the majority of Atlantans. "I had heard of him, but I was only dimly aware of his existence, or of the Braves for that matter."

Mrs. Williams increased Aaron's awareness of black affairs and after meeting her, he began working with Chicago activist, the Rev. Jesse Jackson, and Leon Sullivan, who conceived the Philadelphia Plan of black self-help.

The countdown began in earnest after the 700th home run, but Aaron fans were forced to be patient. There was a 10-day gap between 700 and 701; a 16-day lag from 701 to 702. But he hit three homers in three days from August 16-18 and before the month ended Aaron had nailed down 705 and 706.

He had all of September to hit nine home runs, but tradition was against him. Aaron never hit more than six home runs in September in his 19-year career.

Early in September, however, his bat continued to flame, and on September 3rd, on a tear during which he had driven in 21 runs in the previous 17 games, Aaron hit a pair of home runs in a game in San Diego. No. 707 came off Clay Kirby in the third inning and two innings later, Aaron touched reliever Vicente Romo for 708, his 35 season homers only three behind teammate Dave Johnson, the league leader.

Newspapers all over the country moved their Aaron Barometers, varying typographical gimmicks, to the first sports page. But Aaron continued to tease the public; hitting enough home runs to make it possible he would break the record in 1973, but not enough to make the end of the quest probable.

On September 8th, he hit 709 off Cincinnati's Jack Billingham to break up a scoreless duel. He had 19 games left in which to do or delay. No. 710 came two days later, but there was a week's hiatus before he hit 711 off San Diego's Gary Ross, and there was a five-day delay before 712 came off Houston's Dave Roberts, who in a few days would play a major role in the continuing drama.

An Atlanta university computer had predicted Aaron would not break Ruth's record in 1973, but after he hit

712, Aaron laughed, "I just might mess up that machine a little."

He had six games left to do it, but it took one week and five games to produce 713 and set the stage for one of the more interesting spectacles American sport had ever witnessed.

"I feel like tomorrow is probably going to be the test I've been waiting for all these years," Aaron said after tapping Jerry Reuss for 713 on September 29th. "If I get a pitch to hit, then the world will know if I am a good hitter. I don't want to swing at any bad pitches."

Baseball fans were—it had been demonstrated statistically—hoping Aaron would get his pitch. Days before he got one final shot to put an end to his duel with Ruth in 1973, a Louis Harris poll indicated 68 per cent of all baseball fans said they were "rooting for Hank Aaron of the Atlanta Braves to break Babe Ruth's record of seven-hundred and fourteen lifetime home runs." Further, 87.5 per cent thought "Aaron has been a good player for years and it is good to see him get his due recognition," and 92.3 per cent felt "nearly all records are there to be broken sooner or later, and the lifetime home run record is no exception."

September 30th dawned cloudy in Atlanta, the sky a great, gray dishrag for the Braves' final game of the season and, incidentally, Hank Aaron's last opportunity to escape the spectre of Ruth in the year 1973. Later the sun would beam down briefly on the crowd of 40,517 come to see if Bad Henry could jerk one more out of the ballyard. On the previous nights of this homestand, crowds had averaged less than 5,000, but long lines snaked toward the ticket windows before noon. Far to the north, a wrecking ball was breaking apart Yankee Stadium, the fabled House That Ruth Built with his mighty, bludgeoning bat, but on Peachtree Street the talk was of the erasing of the Babe's finest mark. "The Countdown Is

Among Aaron's staunchest rooters are son Larry and daughter Dorinda. Hank's other children are Gaile and Henry, Jr.

One; Tickets on Sale," glowed the stadium message board.

It was a storybook finish for all time and a nation of history-worshippers held its breadth awaiting the flash: Aaron hits 714. Houston pitcher Dave Roberts did not look forward to being a footnote to the historical smash and tarried in getting to the stadium. When he arrived, a teammate had taped a note to his locker in the Houston clubhouse: "Thanks for Nos. 586, 599, 618, 655, 712, 714 and 715. Hank."

Roberts sought to be deadly serious in pre-game interviews. "I don't want to be the one to give up either the 714th or 715th," said Roberts, who with a win this day could become the first Houston southpaw to ever register 17 victories in a season. "If he comes up at any time with a chance to beat me, I'm going to pitch around him."

The Astros couldn't resist putting the needle in Roberts. Someone took down the number atop his locker and replaced it with the numerals "714," which he promptly switched around to "17" to show the number of wins he sought. But seeing the "714," Roberts, in the vernacular, took the heat. "Talk to Cecil (Upshaw) . . . talk to Jerry (Reuss)," he shouted at reporters, whereupon Houston manager Leo Durocher, involved in the last game of his long career, told writers, "Talk to him after the game. Not now." As the writers left, the disturbed Roberts yelled, "How's Hank taking this?"

Beautifully. As usual. Better than Roberts. Babe Ruth might have had his Tom Zachary. And Roger Maris his Tracy Stallard. But Hank Aaron wasn't going to have Dave Roberts, if the Astro pitcher had anything to say about it. "Everybody kidded me," he said later. "They said 'You'll be famous . . . you'll make the banquet tour all winter . . . you'll get fat by serving a fat pitch. . . .' "

When the game began, the people who had come to witness No. 714 gave Aaron a standing ovation. They were ready. So was Houston pitcher Don Wilson, who had narrowly missed catching No. 713 the night before. He had a glove in one hand and a bat in the other as he stood behind a low fence in the Astro bullpen in center field.

"If a home run came over, I was going to catch it," he explained. "That seven-fourteen would be a valuable baseball." The bat, Wilson said, he would use if the ball were out of reach. "Just like a lacrosse stick."

Standing on the mound, Roberts had a different idea and waved Wilson back to where he belonged. "I was trying to collect my composure," Roberts said. "I didn't want to make a stupid mistake. If he hit it out the first time, I wanted to make sure he hit my best pitch. Waving Wilson back kind of relaxed me."

On his first pitch to Aaron, Roberts grooved a fastball.

There are various schools of thought as to why he came down the pipe. A friend of Aaron's says, "Hank looked at him kind of funny and later he said his kid could've hit that pitch out."

In any case, it was the one pitch Aaron was to see that was suitable for immortality. "He used reverse psychology," Aaron would say later. "I was expecting a changeup. He threw a fastball right down the middle."

"A slider," Roberts argued.

Whatever it was, Aaron pulled it slowly down the third-base line and legged out an infield single. The next time he came to bat, a quartet played "For He's a Jolly Good Fellow," but it served as inspiration for nothing more than a soft single to center, the hit elevating Aaron's average to .300 for the first time in a 1973 season that saw him batting .200 in May.

In the sixth inning, with a light rain falling, Aaron came to the plate again and the message board flashed: "The Hammer's Got the Babe's Number." Obviously, Aaron had Roberts', bouncing a third straight single through the middle. Still he was 0-for-3. Nobody had come to see singles.

Lightning flashed out of a dark sky and rain poured down when Aaron came to the plate after Darrell Evans had struck out in the eighth. Wilson had replaced Roberts on the mound for Houston, a terse announcement in the press box informing writers that "Roberts' shoulder tightened up." Considering Houston owned a 5-1 lead at the time, one wit said perhaps it was Roberts' throat that had tightened.

Whatever the reason, the season and Hank Aaron's bid for a large chunk of immortality was now in the right hand of Wilson. His first pitch was a fastball on the inside corner. Pressure-resistant Hank Aaron finally wilted, lunging after the pitch like a schoolboy. The bat split in half as it made contact with the ball, which at exactly 4:15 p.m. popped feebly into the air just to the left of second base where it became merely a putout.

In Aisle 183, a man arose and shouted baseball's favorite of all cries, "Wait'll next year," and the applause began. It rolled out of the stands and engulfed Aaron; a residue of affection from people who loved him no less for this single failure. Applause fell like the rain for long minutes as Aaron told a television interviewer, "Well, it's over."

And so it was. For awhile. In the Braves' clubhouse, surrounded by a milling horde of reporters, Aaron maintained the cool that had been his trademark throughout his longest season.

"The ovation was tremendous . . . great," he smiled softly, sitting behind no less than 12 microphones the Braves had set up in a special interview room. "I'm sorry I couldn't hit one for them, sitting in the rain and all. I was going for the home run. I wasn't trying to hit singles. And that applause, I guess that's the biggest moment I've ever had in baseball.

"I guess I didn't realize people cared that much.

"I'm disappointed, yes. I tried. The last month was really tension. I feel relieved."

Someone said Babe Ruth had saved baseball and asked Aaron what he thought he had done for the game. It was not a subtle question. Aaron answered it candidly.

"Well, that's a new question. Maybe what I've done is create some new fans for baseball. At first, there was a lot of mail from older people who didn't want me to break Ruth's record. The younger generation took notice of that and came to my support. I think they wanted me to relate to; to see me have a record in their time, not somebody their granddaddies had seen play.

"That's about all I can say I've done for baseball."

When most of the reporters had gone, someone asked Aaron about 1974.

"All I've got to do to get the record is stay alive," he smiled.

Back in the clubhouse proper, Aaron pronounced a last benediction for 1973. "I'm thankful it is over and that it came out as well as it did."

The ghost of Ruth would survive for one more year; and as he had in 1973, Aaron would suffer him well. In short months, they would be asking Babe Who?

Hank and his new bride, Billye, greet well-wishers at a reception in Atlanta.

15

Move Over, Babe

It was, in retrospect, an incredible happenstance. History had stopped one tick short of fulfillment. It was as if Brutus had withheld the dagger an inch from Caesar and gone out for a cigarette before returning to dispatch his mentor; as if Delilah had merely given Samson a light trim. Hank Aaron had moved to the precipice, peered over, and then laid down for a long winter's nap before awakening to leap into immortality.

But whatever the drama of the moment of 714, and its attendant promise of a record falling to earth with the loudest crash the game had ever known, Aaron was never truly chasing a man or a mark. He was in pursuit of a legend, and he was ill-equipped for the chase. He would —because of his lack of flamboyance and because time had invested Ruth with a matchless sheen—never approach the legend, conquering merely a statistic.

Aaron was chasing Ruth only insofar as he might overtake him in the pages of a record book soon to grow mildewed. Ruth the man, Ruth the legendary saviour of the game, Ruth the *star* . . . they would never be within Henry Aaron's grasp.

Even words somehow don't seem adequate to describe Ruth. Where to begin? As a player, he remains peerless, having in a 22-year career established no fewer than 76 major-league records. It is hardly remembered that he began as a pitcher with the Boston Red Sox; that he won 23 games one year, 24 the next and set a World Series record of 29⅔ scoreless innings that stood for 43 years. This, now, was a man history recalls as perhaps its greatest *hitter*.

Certainly Ruth was a hitter. His 60 home runs in 1927—more than hit by any other American League team that year—have never been equalled, Roger Maris' 61 needing an asterisk to gain entry into the baseball ledgers. Ruth's 714 career home runs remained unchallenged by anyone save Aaron. His lifetime batting average was .342 and it is a measure of the man that, asked if he had concentrated on his average could he have closed with a .400 career mark, he replied laughingly, "Hell, kid, I could have hit .500."

But Ruth was far more than a hitter. He was the grandest figure the game has ever known, a totally uninhibited monument of talent and appetite and matchless ability to excite. Damon Runyan in his finest hour could not have invented Ruth, and his effect on baseball is not comparable to that of any other single individual. Sold by the Red Sox to the New York Yankees in 1920 for the then magnificent sum of $125,000, Ruth triggered a wholesale American interest in the game of baseball with his abilities to hit the ball prodigious distances and capture the imagination of both the public and the nation's sportswriters. A pot-bellied, spindly-legged, pigeon-toed giant, he used the home run to transform the game from one of speed and cleverness and guile to one of power. He made the home run a part of our culture, a symbol of our need and affection for the complex issues of the 1920s and '30s to be settled with a single, decisive, quick stroke.

His first season as a Yankee, and no longer a pitcher, he struck 54 home runs, a number exceeding the combined total of 14 of the 15 other major-league teams. Yankee Stadium became "The House That Ruth Built" as American League attendance, 1,708,000 in 1918 before Ruth's bat transfixed the public, ballooned to 5,048,000 in two years. Weaned in a Baltimore saloon and shunted off to a Catholic trade school as "incorrigible" at the age of eight by his bartender-father, Ruth moved baseball to a high noon of popularity and in the process created a mystique, a shadow over the game that never faded. His appetites knew no bounds. Breakfast was a porterhouse steak, four fried eggs, a large portion of fried potatoes, a pot of coffee and a pint of bourbon. Between games of a double-header he would mix a quart of pickled eels supplied by teammate but not necessarily friend Lou Gehrig with a quart of chocolate ice cream. On other days, a half-dozen hot dogs and three quarts of Coke would suffice.

Ruth sought all artifacts of the good life in those quantities: women, luxury cars, booze, food. And, evidence insists unconsciously, he never lacked an anecdote for a reporter. When he demanded and won the unheard of salary of $80,000 in 1930, Ruth was reminded it was $5,000 more than President Herbert Hoover received. "Yeah," yawned the Babe, "but I had a better year."

Celebrities, perhaps because he was ignorant of their accomplishments, never impressed Ruth, who in time became probably the best-known man in the nation. "Hot as hell, ain't it, Prez?" Ruth asked on the sultry day he was introduced to President Calvin Coolidge. And when Marshal Foch, the great French hero of World War I, met Ruth, the Babe shook his hand and said, "Hiya, Gen, you were in the war, huh?"

Portrayed as something of a buffoon over the years, Ruth protested to a reporter, "I'm no clown. I'm really a serious guy. I read books. Why don't you ask me about books for a change." The reporter said, "all right, what do you think of the Napoleonic era?" Snapped Ruth, "I think it should have been scored as a hit."

As his home runs came to number in the hundreds, Ruth gained a fame that would never yield to a mere numbers game perpetrated by any man so lacking in charisma as Hank Aaron. In Mobile, they tell a story, probably apocryphal, that pictures the impact the Babe made on the culture. "Ruth played here one time," Herbert Aaron Sr. recalled. "I didn't see him, but some of my friends said he hit a home run into an open coal car going by the ballpark and that some guy found it in New Orleans."

Those were the sort of tales engendered by Ruth's bat and his personality: the sort of a bastille Aaron could never storm in any quest to become known as the greatest home run hitter in history.

Ironically, with the glare on Aaron's 714th home run, Ruth's issued forth undramatized on a rainy day in Pittsburgh while he was suffering the first stages of cancer and nearly blind in one eye. The Yankees had traded him to the Boston Braves of the National League in the winter of 1934 after insulting him by mailing him a contract for one dollar. With Boston, he was to be vice president, assistant manager and rightfielder. He celebrated his 40th birthday the day after Aaron's first one. The power had not dried up, but the swing had slowed badly and his legs were gone and he was undeniably fat. Ruth was struggling when the Braves pulled into Pittsburgh on May 24th, 1935. That night, he got drunk and stayed out on the town until 5 A.M. with a Pittsburgh sportswriter who the next day informed Pirate manager Pie Traynor, "Don't worry about Babe. He and I were out all night."

That day Ruth struck his last three home runs; No. 714 a prodigious shot that was the first ball to ever clear the skyscraper right field stands at Forbes Field. He had destroyed the Pirates in four straight games in the 1927 World Series and on this one day, it had all come back. Later, he said, "For one day I again wore the crown."

It was the last game he ever played and when it became clear he was finished, Ruth told friends he thought 714 would stand forever. The evidence insisted he was right. The previous career home run record belonged to one Roger Connor, a left-handed third baseman who hit 131 during an 18-year career that ended in 1898.

But there are those of the opinion that Ruth would've applauded Aaron's effort. One of them is, of course, his widow, Claire Ruth. Another one is former St. Louis Brown pitcher Bobo Newsom, who told a story that wasn't necessarily true but sounded an awful lot like the Babe. Newsom was pitching the final game of the 1938 season against Detroit and Hank Greenberg, who had 58 home runs going into the last day of the year. "I got a telegram that morning," Newsom said. "It said, 'records are made to be broken. Bear down.' It was signed Babe Ruth. That afternoon I struck out the gentleman (Greenberg) three times."

Claire Ruth, a beautiful young model and actress when she married and partially tamed Ruth in 1929, seemed irked by comparisons of her husband's feat and Aaron's but she said in the spring of 1974, "I'll be cheering for Mr. Aaron and I know the Babe would be cheering for him, too, if he were here."

Sitting in the huge apartment she and Ruth shared on Riverside Drive in New York City, Claire Ruth is her husband's greatest champion. "Every homer Babe hit brought them out of their seats. The Babe loved baseball so much, I'm sure he would've been pulling for Hank

Aaron to break his record. He would've enjoyed watching him try."

Mrs. Ruth's father was Ty Cobb's lawyer, and she and Johnny Mize are cousins, so she was no baseball novice when she met Ruth. But she, too, was caught up in his legend. "The Babe hit all of his homers in 14 years. I think it is ridiculous for Hank Aaron to be compared with him. After all, Babe pitched his first six years and didn't get to bat as much. And now there's been expansion, there are 162 games played where Babe played in only 154. Hank's been to bat over 10,000 times . . . Babe batted only a little over 8,000.

"It's like I have been saying. People remember the man who flew over the Atlantic the first time. There have been several since Lindbergh, but he's the only one they remember."

No one had to tell Aaron there was only one Lindbergh, only one Babe. "When they talk about home runs, they'll say Babe Ruth, Henry Aaron, in that order . . . I don't think I'll get nearly the acclaim that came along with his home runs. The public as a whole will always remember Babe Ruth."

By 1974, Aaron's tone toward Ruth had gone from disinterest to tolerance. "Why should I have read about a man playing a game that I couldn't get into at the time," Aaron said when he first became a threat to Ruth. Then he had no hero save Jackie Robinson. "Ruth was in a different world. Baseball when he played was something no black kid could relate to. Of all the pictures I ever saw of Ruth, I never saw one of him with any black kids."

As an equal, he spoke a different tune. "I've grown to admire Babe Ruth. Anytime a ballplayer can hit as many home runs as he did in so short a time he must've been something special."

Apparently the American public considered Henry Aaron something special, too. The 1973 off-season brought remarkable riches to a man who was still fond of reminiscing over a poor, colored boy who left Mobile with two dollars. As he had hidden his divorce from the public, so did Aaron hide his second marriage. He and Billye Williams—who had inadvertently divulged their engagement on her television show by wearing her ring—slipped off to Jamaica and were married there the first week in November. The ten-minute ceremony, in the lovely chapel of the University of the West Indies, was witnessed by Gaile Aaron and Mrs. Williams' only child, Deidre, 6, and Jamaican tourism minister Eric Abrahams and his wife, who had lured the couple to Jamaica with the promise their wedding would be kept secret. They honeymooned a week in a private villa on Jamaica.

"We both had adjustment problems of our own when we met," the new Mrs. Aaron said. "He had just been divorced, I was a recent widow. But gradually our friendship grew stronger and stronger."

Billye Aaron, used to the spotlight, was not enamored of it. "I hope he hits the home runs and then the attention will fizzle out. You can be big in the news one day and out of it the next, and that's good. It would be awful to keep up this current pace."

But it was to be awhile before the pace would die down. For one thing, Hank Aaron had first to become a millionaire. That happened on January 21st, 1974 in a private dining room at Jimmy's, a New York restaurant the Magnavox Corporation chose to introduce its newest acquisition to the press.

Standing at the podium, his hands shaking slightly, Henry Aaron looked straight ahead as a man from Magnavox issued a startling statement: "We're happy to announce a long-term, comprehensive association with Henry Aaron that will mean one million dollars to him over a period of the next five years."

Henry Aaron, who in his day had gone from hand-me-downs to Peachtree Street bankers' clothing that put him on America's "10-best-dressed men" list, had it made. Later when he walked out of Jimmy's into the sunlight, he would tell the man from Magnavox, over and over, "I just can't believe it." And even later, when he returned to Mobile and a taste of Estella Aaron's cooking, he would say to his family, "Imagine . . . me making a million dollars."

In fact, his assault on the record would be worth considerably more than a million. According to Berle Adams, president of WMA Sports, Inc., a subsidiary of the William Morris Talent Agency which was handling Aaron's financial affairs, the record would be worth considerably more. In time, Aaron would apply his soft sell in behalf of automobiles, food and beverage products, men's deodorants and, of course, a variety of Magnavox products.

In signing Aaron to the million-dollar contract, Magnavox was taking a calculated risk. The company's stock in recent years had dropped from $18 to $7 a share and it desperately needed a new public image, which it hoped Aaron would help provide. "He's a hero at a time when America is looking for a hero," was the way the company put it.

"With the record being broken, it's worth at least $4 million to $5 million of additional income over the next few years," said Aaron's personal financial advisor, Frank Menke.

"If I don't hit another baseball, my kids will be able to go to college and I'll be able to eat," Aaron low-keyed his new wealth. He found it hard to accept the fact that people were pushing money at him from every direction. He was black. How many white people would be moved to purchase products endorsed by a black? Aaron had made only $18,000 the previous year from such activities, but as he neared the record he realized the need for the

Before the '74 season Aaron films a commercial at Atlanta Stadium for his sponsor, Magnavox.

type of guidance only a man such as Berle Adams could provide. "He was really uptight the first time we met," Adams said. "The first thing he asked me was, 'How much do I have to give up?' "

"Give up?" Adams asked.

"In income, because I'm black."

"If you asked me ten years ago, I'd have said 60 per cent. Today, maybe 20 to 25 per cent."

Later, Adams told Aaron being black apparently would not cost him a dime in the marketplace. "We didn't have to give up one cent," Adams reported. "He got the biggest deal Magnavox ever negotiated for a professional athlete."

Rich, recently wed, relaxed and 40, Hank Aaron went to spring training to prepare for the disposition of the record unaware he would become the center of one of the bigger baseball controversies in recent years. The other participants were Brave owner Bill Bartholomay, Commissioner Bowie Kuhn, and to a lesser extent, general manager Eddie Robinson, field manager Eddie Mathews, and an aroused, even indignant sporting press.

The passion play began to unfold in Jimmy's restaurant the day Aaron signed with Magnavox. "I would like the 714th and 715th home runs to be hit in Atlanta," Aaron said. Plagued by the Braves' slump at the gate in recent years, Bartholomay heartily concurred. But there was a rub: Atlanta was scheduled to open the season with three games in Cincinnati. Aaron and Bartholomay agreed on a solution. "I've talked it over with Bill Bartholomay and I think I'll play the second game in Cincinnati and sit out the other two," Aaron said.

As he readied himself for the season at his own pace—"he knows what he has to do; I don't have to tell him," said Mathews—controversy swirled.

Led by New York writers, the press assailed the Braves' plan to withhold Aaron from the game for the

Hank cooks up something with his wife and hostess Dinah Shore on the TV show, "Dinah's Place."

How times have changed! Lieut. Governor Lester Maddox sits beside the Aarons as the Georgia general assembly pays tribute to Hank.

purpose of making history in Atlanta the following Monday night in a nationally-televised game. Dave Anderson of *The New York Times*—one of the most widely-respected writers in the nation—wrote without rancor:

"Henry Aaron isn't appearing in a concert. He's a member of a competitive baseball team. In their concentration on the home run record, he and the Braves' owner appear to have forgotten the integrity of the situation. If the Braves adhere to the competitive mandate of putting their best lineup on the field, it's imperative the 40-year-old Aaron play in the opener, assuming he's healthy."

Anderson's observations apparently were logical to Kuhn, the usually ineffectual commissioner thought lacking the power or fortitude to buck management. But Kuhn balked at Bartholomay's plan to commercialize history. They talked several times at length. Finally, the week before the opener, Kuhn released a statement that was in effect both an order and a swat at the Brave owner. It read, in part, "I have advised him (Bartholomay) that I am disapproving the announcement and that, barring disability, I will expect the Braves to use Henry Aaron in the opening series in Cincinnati in accordance with the pattern of his use in 1973 when he started approximately two of every three Braves' games."

Aaron's reaction was not typical. He wondered aloud if "the commissioner was going to make out Cincinnati's lineup, too. I live in Atlanta. That's where I want to hit the home run that ties the record and the one that breaks the record. I still believe I owe it to the Atlanta fans."

But finally he acquiesced to Kuhn's order. "If the commissioner says I gotta play, I gotta play," he told the horde of reporters who trailed him daily during spring training. "I'm ready to get this thing over."

It was an understatement of magnificent proportion. Indeed, Henry Aaron was ready. The Braves opened the

1974 season in Cincinnati a day after the city was devastated by a tornado which killed five and caused more than $15 million in damages. Henry Aaron immediately visited Cincinnati with another sort of plague.

In the first inning of the first game on the first swing of his 21st season, Aaron hit No. 714. Cincinnati's Jack Billingham, who had given up four previous Aaron home runs, fed him a sinking fastball on a 3-1 count with two men on. The pitch was meant to tail away from Aaron; grab the outside corner Billingham had managed to nick on only one of four earlier deliveries. It did not sink fast enough or far enough. "A mistake," Billingham sighed later, "and Henry Aaron hits mistakes."

Aaron swung his 34¾ ounce, 33½ inch white ash bat and hit this mistake approximately 400 feet. Suddenly, at 2:37 P.M. on an overcast afternoon, all the conflict and controversy and pressure disappeared. With the crack of the bat, Cincinnati left fielder Pete Rose had broken for the fence at the 350-foot mark in the left-center power alley. When he ran out of room, he stopped and watched the ball clear the 12-foot fence by about three feet. It hit a wall behind the fence and was retrieved on one hop by Clarence Williams, a Cincinnati policeman disguised in the red cap and uniform of a groundskeeper who would later be compensated by both clubs. Aaron did not watch the flight of the historic home run. "I never watch them; I leave that for the umpires." NBC-TV immediately interrupted the continuing problems of Alice, Rachael and Lenore on the afternoon soap opera "Another World" and flashed an instant replay to 8.5 million viewers.

As the number 714 lit up the scoreboard, Hank Aaron circled the bases as he had on 713 previous occasions—slowly but a bit jauntily, head up, elbows back. He made a prophet of Cincinnati manager Sparky Anderson, who

In his first time at bat in the 1974 season's opener, Hank Aaron hit No. 714 off the Reds' Jack Billingham to tie Babe Ruth's record.

said before the game, "he's so calm, he won't do anything different." This time Aaron permitted himself a small smile as he crossed the plate, where pitcher Ron Reed stood grinning hugely, a clenched fist thrust toward the sky.

The Riverfront Stadium sellout crowd of 52,134 fans, which included Vice President Gerald Ford and the governor of Ohio, had been stunned into silence by the suddenness of the home run. When the shock wore off, it erupted and there was a great outpouring of a kind of love. He had made them a part of history and their thanks was long minutes in spending itself. Baseball fans who couldn't be present sent their gratitude in a deluge of telegrams which Western Union predicted would set an all-time record for messages sent to an individual.

As Aaron trotted to the plate—"when I hit the next one I'll probably run around the bases backwards"—the Braves had streamed from their dugout while the Reds appeared almost transfixed. Aaron was engulfed in a cloud of patting hands and hugs, the celebration carrying him back toward the dugout. He broke free and moved to a box seat next to the Atlanta dugout and lifted his face. Billye Aaron, sitting with her in-laws, leaned down and kissed her husband long and hard, as Herbert Aaron Sr. slapped frantically at his son and grinned the grin of a man come to some unbelievably satisfying moment. "I didn't say anything," Aaron said later. "I was just happy they were there to see this home run."

Williams and another policeman, Steve Halpin, escorted the historic ball back to the infield. Umpire John McSherry intercepted them near second base and hurried the ball to Aaron, nervously pacing among his milling teammates in the Brave dugout. Meanwhile, Vice President Ford and Commissioner Kuhn moved onto the playing field and Aaron jogged to meet them. "Good luck for 715 and many more. It's a great day for you, a great day for baseball," Ford said to Aaron, who then was given a trophy by Kuhn and a plaque commemorating the event by Bartholomay.

A microphone was brought out and Aaron spoke briefly but sincerely to the crowd. "I'd certainly like to thank you. I'm just glad it's almost over with."

Aaron had three more opportunities to break the record, but the ghost of Ruth held sway for a few more days. Aaron grounded to third in the third inning, walked on four pitches in the fifth when the crowd rained boos on Billingham, and then lined out to center in the seventh off reliever Roger Nelson. With the Braves ahead, 6-2, he was removed in the seventh, a customary practice in deference to his advanced years.

When it was over—Cincinnati rallied to win, 7-6, in the 11th when Pete Rose scored all the way from second base on a wild pitch—Aaron remained what he has always been. A quiet, dignified, pleasant man.

"Tying the record is great, but breaking it is another thing," he said in a stuffy interview room awash with reporters. "I thought tying the record would mean a lot to me, but it's just another home run. It's a load off my back. I feel like it's really over now. But some of the edge was rubbed off because we lost, otherwise I'd be in the clubhouse right now drinking champagne."

The champagne was there, but Aaron ordered it remain uncorked. It had been, despite all his calm and cool, a trying day. To observers, he had been imperturbable, but he admitted he "had been a little uptight before the game." And during batting practice, he had whispered to teammate Dave Johnson, "am I swinging all right . . . do I look OK?" Johnson had smiled. "Yes, kid, you look OK." "Do I look nervous?" Johnson's smile widened. "Yeah, you look nervous." The feeling hadn't passed when the game was over and he had knocked at least one of Ruth's feet off the pedestal.

And there was the matter of the tribute to Dr. Martin Luther King, assassinated six years ago on that date. Before the game, Aaron had talked with civil rights leader Dr. Jesse Jackson, and then he and the other Braves had asked Cincinnati officials to observe a moment of silence in King's memory. The request was refused, although later no one would admit having made the decision. "For some reason, they said their schedule wouldn't permit it," Aaron observed rather bitterly. "I was very disappointed." So was Billye Aaron, who said "it shouldn't have been necessary to request a moment of silence."

In the Cincinnati clubhouse and elsewhere, those who had some piece of the action had their own thoughts. Jack Billingham, whose wife had sought out and congratulated Billye Aaron, was matter of fact. "I'll give up 25 home runs this year and he got the first one," Billingham said. A 31-year-old veteran who had been tapped for Aaron homers Nos. 528, 636, 641 and 709, he was neither distraught or unconcerned about becoming an historic figure. "I don't want to leave my mark on the game that way," he said. He had felt that way a long time. In 1973, asked if he would enjoy being Aaron's Guy Bush, Billingham had been emphatic. "I wouldn't try to give it up to him," he had said then. "If I had a 14-0 lead and Aaron was up, I'd still be careful. I wouldn't walk him in that situation. But I'd make him hit my pitch —no fastball."

Yes, Billingham sighed, it had been a fastball that Aaron had hit. "It was going toward the outside of the plate . . . but it tailed in. That's what makes Aaron great. He hits mistakes."

In Jacksonville, Florida, Billingham's sister thought "the homer will bother him a little, but in 15 years, when he's out of baseball, he'll be proud of it." Jack Billingham was not so sure. Bumping into Aaron later, he said "congratulations . . . but why'd you have to hit it off me?"

Billingham, nicknamed "Fat Jack," seemed truly displeased by becoming history's handmaiden, although before the game he had said, "I don't feel he can hit a home run off me if I get my sinker where I want it, but I wouldn't care if he hit four as long as we won. The number 714 really isn't in my mind."

It was, however, in the minds of Herbert Aaron Sr. ("I knew he would hit one today 'cause it was so warm") and Billye Aaron ("This is nerve-wracking . . . he'll be damned if he hits it and damned if he doesn't").

And it had been in the mind of Henry Aaron, who was perhaps weary of the charge that he had no appreciation of high drama. "I felt before the game I was going to hit one," he said. And then he smiled softly, possibly recalling the time he had been said to lack Ruth's elan, Ruth's flair, Ruth's grasp on the fan. But in all of Ruth's years, Aaron must've known, he had never authored quite so thrilling a home run.

"I'm just sorry you gentlemen didn't see the other one today," Aaron said as he was about to leave the interview room. "But it will come."

It did.

Clip and Mail This Special Shipping Label and...

Let these Get-Ahead books help you write better, read faster, speak more effectively!

Here's an unusual opportunity for everyone who is determined to get ahead in business, socially or at school. Just print your name and address on the special shipping label printed on the opposite page. Clip it out and mail it together with the coupon below. We will paste your label on a package containing six valuable get-ahead books jam-packed with the powerful ideas, practical helps and short-cut steps you need for improving your writing, reading and speaking skills right now. These books cost $27.30 in their original hard-covers. Now, they're yours for only $5.45 in practical paperbacks. Here's a brief glimpse of what you get:

(1) Better Writing
Shows how to get your thoughts on paper easily, quickly, more clearly and forcefully.

(2) Faster Reading
Proven-successful ways to increase your reading speed and help you understand and remember more.

(3) Increase Your Vocabulary
How to expand your vocabulary quickly. 30-day new-word-mastery technique.

(4) Synonyms & Antonyms Dictionary
Provides exact words you need to express your written and spoken thoughts. Easy to use.

(5) Reference Guide
Leads you through the maze of almanacs, encyclopedias, atlases, manuals, and all other reference materials.

(6) Desk Dictionary
664 pages of clear, complete, up-to-date definitions, pronunciations, usages, origins of words. Illustrated.

MAIL THIS COUPON WITH SHIPPING LABEL NOW